Sex, Drugs and Digging a Hole

Heather McCarthy

Copyright ©© 2013 Heather McCarthy

The names and places have been changed to protect the innocent

All rights reserved.

No part of this book may be reproduced without written permission from the author.

ISBN: 1499598548
ISBN-13: 978-1499598544

DEDICATION

William Daley

To my husband for whom this story could not be possible
without his resources and continued encouragement.

CONTENTS

	Acknowledgments	i
1	The End	1
2	The Chase is On	19
3	The Early Months	35
4	Progressions	51
5	Holes	73
6	California Disaster	95
7	Home Again	123
8	Neighbors	155
9	Wigging Out	175
10	Buried	197
11	The Beginning	221
12	The Caribbean	237
	Epilogue	269

ACKNOWLEDGMENTS

Elaborate confessions and experiences from various friends.

Todd Larson, Editor

Gina P.
Cover Photography

Kristin J.
Cover Model

THE END

In the early hours of a December morning, Ryan O'Connor rolled over to Amy's side of the bed and softly brushed the auburn hair from her lethargic face. He kissed her neck and slowly moved down her breastbone, making sure to stop and suckle on her lovely round nipples as he aroused her from a sound sleep.

"Ryan, stop it," she protested, pushing his head away from her breast.

Amy, definitely not a morning person, never saw the break of dawn. Although she had just begun the rehabilitation process, most times she rose from the bed in a zombielike stupor with a head of frizz, her emerald eyes encased in dark circles.

"Come on, Amy. Just a quickie before breakfast," he urged as he tried to hold her naked body close to him for just a few more seconds.

"No, I had a long night, and I'm hung over," she told him firmly. "I need coffee! Let's play after breakfast." She rolled over and threw the covers from her naked body.

Ryan's niece had married her high-school sweetheart, and the party lasted until midnight. It had been a long time since they had accepted family invitations.

Amy rose from the satin sheets and dragged her feet to the kitchen to make coffee. She tried to fill the carafe with water, but the high stack of greasy pots and dirty dishes blocked the spigot. She moved to the bathroom sink, turned on the faucet, and filled the carafe. Back in the kitchen, she poured the water in the coffee pot and flipped the switch with a flick of her finger.

Thinking only of the pounding in her head, she grabbed the bottle of Excedrin on the windowsill. She fumbled with the childproof cap and, dispensing two, swallowed them dry.

"Is the coffee ready yet?" Ryan asked, heavy-eyed, as he walked into the kitchen with strands of flaxen hair dangling over slanted eyebrows. He was tall, bare-chested, and sexy. Her neck and arms tingled as she sensed his piercing blue eyes staring through her tousled hair and makeup-free face. "You look beautiful this morning," he told her.

"Thanks," she said loosely. "I just poured the water. It should be ready shortly." Staring at Ryan with a trivial smile, she remembered how perfect life had been in the beginning and wondered why she had allowed their circumstances to get so out of hand.

"Want me to start breakfast?" he asked as he slowly moved to the refrigerator.

"Oh, yes, I'm starving," she said. "A little salt and grease should take the edge off this hangover." She opened the kitchen cabinet and clutched the blue cup for Ryan and the monogrammed vessel for herself. She removed the breakfast plates to the left of the coffee cups and the silverware from the drawer, and arranged everything on the kitchen table. She thought about nothing except the emptiness in her stomach.

The compact room contained everything essential for any kitchen: a new stove, refrigerator and microwave. She was constantly nudging elbows with him as she passed through the tight space. Opening the refrigerator door, he removed the bacon. He picked up four eggs and gently placed them on the stove.

As Ryan sizzled the bacon and cracked the eggs over the frying pan, the aroma of salty meat, grease and Folgers coffee filled the room, causing her hangover to subside. He stood tall and half-naked at the stove, flipping the eggs and humming a song. He had an enchanting voice, and she loved to listen to him sing, except when she was nursing a headache.

"I know how to fix you right up," he said with a willing smile as she watched him engulf his breakfast. She loved everything about him. She smiled, knowing he was a part of her life. His foolish sense of humor and contagious laugh made her comfortable and self-assured.

"Really, and what might that be?" she inquired with a frown. She wanted to wait until her breakfast had stuck to the lining of her stomach. She had no illusions about his desires, and she knew from the tone of his voice what he wanted.

"Are you ready for some morning delight?" He stared at her and waited for an answer, but she ignored him. "Take a long hot shower and we can fool around," he continued, with a sultry tone. "You told me after coffee and breakfast."

She parted her lips in a fake smile and ignored him once again. She tried not to arouse him, because her eyes still quivered from the sunlight shining through the window. "My head is still pounding, and I need another cup of coffee to get the ice out of my bones." She paused thoughtfully. "Maybe a little later."

Rising from the table, she walked to the kitchen sink and added the breakfast dishes to the growing stack. Ryan approached her from behind and stroked her silky hair, sweeping it from her neck. He bent down and kissed her neck softly. He reached around to her breasts and cupped them in his supple masculine hands. They fit perfectly.

Her body warmed and quivered from his touch. She clutched his hands. "Wait a minute, let me take a shower. I'll meet you in the bedroom," she said, running her fingertip down his smooth chest. "I guess a little naughty sex might help."

She walked into the bathroom and turned on the shower. She let the water run until it became hot enough for her to bear. She undressed and stepped into the tub. With perfumed soap she lathered her voluptuous breasts. She slid the soap down between her thighs and around to her buttocks.

She turned her back to the showerhead, allowing the steamy water to pulsate on her head and neck. Her headache slowly cleared as she turned off the shower, stepped out of the tub, and wrapped a cozy bath towel around her wet and naked body.

As she reached the bedroom, Ryan stood naked beside the bed. He tugged on her towel, and as it fell to the floor, he gently pushed her shoulders. She fell backwards on the bed with her feet dangling off the side.

"Are you ready for me?" he asked with longing in his bedroom eyes. He stood statuesque with certainty above her. She nodded her head in agreement as he knelt down, facing her, and spread her legs. With her legs four feet apart, he lifted her calves and placed them on his robust shoulders. "Slide down closer to me," he demanded. Her buttocks slid naturally on the sapphire satin sheets. He nudged his head in between her thighs until his face and mouth rested on her ginger pubes. His long tongue circled her clit round and round until she became wet. He licked his way to her vagina, and it darkened with her arousal. He pushed his succulent tongue in and out, torturing her. "Do you want me to make you cum?" he whispered softly in her musky scent.

"Oh, yes. Please," she begged with a moan. He pushed his tongue inside her, softer and faster until she groaned in ecstasy. A strident scream escaped her lips, and then another, as she reached a splendid orgasm from a simply superb tongue.

"Now it's my turn," Ryan uttered with a familiar sexy voice she understood. He released her legs and lay beside her on the bed. "Let's try something different," he smiled brazenly. Ryan gently pushed her into a half turn while she slid easily on the satin sheets. Her curly locks smothered his chiseled face, and her lips engulfed his cock. Using her lips, she stroked up and down slowly.

He blew on her clit once again, and she moaned. "Faster," he told her, "do it faster." She slid her mouth up and down faster. He licked the opening of her vagina and slid his tongue deep inside her.

She sucked harder and harder until he became stiff. He licked her clit again until she came once more. She let out a quivering scream and a sigh of relief. He mounted her and thrust his penis deep inside her juicy center as they both screamed in rapture.

Amy relaxed and stroked Ryan's chest beneath the satin sheets as he began to snore. She waited for Ryan to drift into a shallow sleep and slipped out of bed, throwing a silk robe over her naked form. She shuffled to the kitchen sink and turned the faucet on. She started to rinse the stack of soiled dishes when the telephone rang. She hurried to the phone in her stocking feet, trying not to wake Ryan. On the second ring, she lifted the handset.

"Hello," she mumbled, still shaky from her hangover and orgasm.

"Amy?" a familiar voice asked, and one she did

not want to hear. "You don't sound too good. Are you sick?"

"I'm okay," she rudely replied, trying to keep the conversation short. "Hold on." She placed the handset down on the coffee table, scurried to the kitchen, and poured another cup of coffee. She returned to the phone, placed it against her high cheekbone and asked frostily, "What can I do for you?"

"I have bad news. Dad died last night in his sleep," he told her, seeming to be in control. She always knew it was difficult for her brother to show his emotions, especially to her. He usually spoke to her in a condescending manner, and made jokes she did not find funny. He loved to be sarcastic and always made fun of her nose. He introduced her to his friends as "his melancholy sister" with "a head like a melon" and "a face like a collie." She hated him.

Her heart began to palpitate, and her breathing lacked depth. The handset slipped from her trembling hand. A tear streamed down her soft cheek to the corner of her coral lip. She wanted to vomit.

"Hello? Hello?" the receiver repeated. She opened her mouth and tried to form words, but nothing flowed.

The ring of the telephone had awaken Ryan. He hollered from the bedroom, "Who is it?" There was no response, and he yelled again, "Amy, what the hell? Who are you talking to?"

She realized soon after that he had not yelled, but just spoke in his usual manner. She had never been the silent type. She always said something, whether it was good or bad.

With the unexpected silence in the apartment, he slid out of bed, pulled his pants over his strapping buttocks, and entered the living room, where Amy was standing, tall but doubtful, in shock. "What the hell, what's the matter with you?" he demanded. She lowered her soggy eyes to the handset on the floor. Ryan, standing half-naked, bent down and picked it up.

"Hello," he said curiously into the handset. "Who is this?"

"Hello, is that you, Ryan?"

"Yeah, it's me," he responded, immediately recognizing the voice of Amy's brother.

She strolled to the butcher-block table, placed the coffee cup down, and sat in her favorite chair. Propping her elbows on the table and cupping her freckled face in her palms, she began to snivel. Her wispy hair fell across the sides of her face and her pale, freckled arms.

She listened as Ryan discussed with her brother the details of the funeral arrangements, which included a prayer service on Wednesday and a funeral mass on Thursday. Breathing in a whiff of coffee, she heaved a sigh and thought about what a selfish asshole her brother had been over the last two years.

Amy's relationship with her brother was as turbulent as a New England Nor'easter and ferocious as a Florida hurricane for most of their childhood. Sibling rivalry seemed to be the root of their mutual dislike, but their relationship grew hostile when he moved their father to Florida without her consent. Over the years, she had learned he only thought of himself and the things he wanted. With the death of their father, he became her last living relative. Her mother had died three years earlier.

She kept her drug addiction secret and knew it could not be a contributing factor to their mutual dislike. Her father's sudden death aroused a variety of emotions in her. His total estate amounted to five hundred thousand dollars, and she knew her brother would fight for the inheritance. The money was never an issue for her, but the bills were three months behind, and they owed sixty thousand to the Internal Revenue Service. The terms of her father's will would not be known for another three years.

She thought about the last twenty years with Ryan and the choices she made. "Maybe it was a mistake to marry Ryan?" she whispered across the table.

Amy wiped another tear from her cheek. She thought about buying new clothes for the funeral because all her dresses had outdated and her high heels had nicks and scratches. She had no cash available, and this would force her to borrow money from her sister-in-law. *They had borrowed so much money over the years,* she thought to herself. *What would be the harm in another fifty?* She would call Ryan's sister the next day, check out Wal-Mart, and call work to schedule a bereavement leave.

Amy worked at the Presidential Hotel in Quincy, Massachusetts, as an assistant manager. She held a bachelor's degree in business administration. The position opened avenues for interacting with all types of stimulating guests, and it made her job exciting. She dealt with a few celebrities, many politicians, and families on vacation.

Even though Amy and Ryan's combined earnings came to ninety thousand a year, the money they earned went to the devil.

Oh, yes, the devil indeed...

First thing Monday morning, Amy showered and dressed as she wiped away her sniffles. Meanwhile, Ryan drove to his sister's house to borrow more money. He returned within the hour and took her shopping at Wal-Mart. Amy chose a sable dress with white lapels and black shoes with two-inch-high heels. She paid the salesperson forty-nine dollars and thanked her.

At eight o'clock Wednesday morning, Ryan and Amy left the apartment, dressed in tasteful black. She wore her new dress, and he had settled on a handsome but worn-out black suit. It was the only one he owned, and she had bought it for him just before their wedding.

In the pouring rain Amy cried all the way to the funeral home. By the time they arrived, her tears had dried. She survived the prayer service as respectfully as she could and avoided superfluous conversation with her brother.

As she stood in the peaceful, loving arms of Ryan, she reminisced about the day she had met him, and her thoughts drifted back in time to all their old habits...

* * *

Amy met Ryan O'Connor at the age of thirty-six when his sister introduced them on a snowy night in December at Excelsior, an upscale nightclub in downtown Boston. She dated him for ten months before he finally proposed on a colorful New England autumn day, when the leaves had reached their splendid peak. Ryan, five years younger, was everything any woman could hope for, and she fell madly in love with him, as he did with her. Their love was unconditional. Ryan married Amy the following September and furnished an immense two-bedroom apartment in historic Quincy.

On an enchanting New England coastline, the City of Presidents is rich in historical treasures and complements Boston beautifully as tourists take a boardwalk stroll of the scenic Marina Bay area. On hot summer nights, the spectacular yellow-orange sun slowly falls on the cool water over Boston Harbor and heightens the incredible view of the Boston skyline from Marina Bay.

* * *

Amy's first encounter with drugs occurred her senior year of high school when she smoked her first marijuana cigarette—"a joint." She sucked on the combination of shredded leaf and flower buds wrapped in twisted white paper that emanates the funky odor familiar to rock concerts. As she exhaled the smoke, she forcibly choked, which sent her into a brash coughing fit. Her head swam, and her body floated like a leaf on a fall breeze. She laughed at nothing in particular, and her sense of time faded away. She craved a Whopper, French fries and a milkshake, even though she never ate at fast-food restaurants. She became limp at first, but soon trembled with anxiety and paranoia. Her body turned to mush. She hated the loss of control and the dulling sensation the "pot" created. She decided not to smoke pot again.

When she reached her first year of college, her friend Judy suggested a line—cocaine.

"You know how to snort, don't you?" Judy asked with a quirky smile. She had a weight problem all of her life, but almost everyone overlooked it because of her spry personality.

Amy lowered her head in embarrassment. "As a matter of fact, I never used cocaine, but watched friends snort at parties," she replied. "I heard it is a great feeling and always wanted to try, but nobody ever offered." She looked down and glanced at the little pile of white powder Judy had placed on a small mirror. Using a credit card from her purse, Judy divided the pile into six separate three-inch lines. She opened her wallet, removed a twenty-dollar bill, and rolled it into a straw.

"Do you do this often?" Amy asked.

Judy rubbed her nose and said, "I snort once in a while, and I'll show you exactly what to do." She bent her full-figured body down over the mirror. In three swift snorts she inhaled three lines, leaving the other three for Amy. "It's easy—now do what I did," she instructed her friend.

Amy bent her aquiline nose over the mirror and duplicated Judy's movements. Within minutes her heart raced and pummeled, as if bursting from her chest. Her body twitched. Her eyes stretched wide, and her energy levels soared to unimaginable heights. She picked up the clutter of magazines on the table and flicked through them in the fast-forward motion of a videocassette recorder. She rearranged them in a neat pile. She reached for another magazine and scrolled the pages in five seconds. She quickly switched from the magazine to solitaire, turning the cards rapidly as Judy lit another cigarette from the one already in her mouth.

Now Amy loved everything cocaine had to offer. She continued her coke-snorting habit in a social capacity until she met Ryan—for she knew when to quit, and addiction had never entered her mind.

* * *

Meanwhile, Ryan started smoking pot at Braintree High School at the age of sixteen. On Friday nights he hung out with friends and drank beers at the baseball field. His friends turned him on to his first joint.

He snorted his first line of cocaine in his tenth year of high school during a class ski trip to Vermont and continued to do so after high school. His older friends, Bobby and Dave, progressed to the next level of euphoria with crack and introduced Ryan one step closer to shaking the devil's hand.

On an August weekend, as the three of them partied at a friend's cottage in Yarmouth, a quaint Yankee town in Cape Cod, Bobby and Dave pointed him toward a crawlspace about four feet high beneath the cottage floor. His friends chose this peculiar spot to avoid attention. They knew not everyone would be cool with coke.

Grabbing a couple of milk crates from the side of the cottage to sit on, Bobby removed a glass pipe from his inside vest pocket. He softly placed a rock of crack cocaine in the bowl of the pipe. Bobby smoked first. He handed the pipe to Dave, who took his hit. Dave looked directly at Ryan. "Are you ready for the ride of your life?" he asked, as he handed the pipe to Ryan.

"Let's rock and roll!" Ryan said gleefully. He placed his lips to the pipe and inhaled the strong demon blend. A strange metamorphose twisted him into a different creature. His face turned blank, his eyes bulged as though leaving his sockets, and his mouth opened wide with a slight drool. As time evolved, this became the longest ride of their lives.

* * *

On a windy Sunday night in September, after returning from a honeymoon cruise in St. Maarten, Ryan and Amy began a life together. The moment their eyes met, they were madly in love and looked ahead for happy times. The only responsibility they lacked was the caring of children, but they decided not to have any before the wedding.

Heather McCarthy

THE CHASE IS ON

Whether it is the streets of Roxbury, Dorchester, or Quincy, he cruised the cities south of Boston during the hours of noon and midnight. Born in Haiti, Junior immigrated to the United States shortly after his eighteenth birthday. After arriving in the United States, he quickly learned legitimate nine to five jobs did not satisfy his goals the way selling the devil's product did. Once his friends exposed him to a life of drugs, he made a substantial living as a dealer. He earned enough money to afford designer clothing, expensive cars, and fine-looking women.

On a tepid night, in early September, as winds from a tropical storm rose to a howl, Junior's cell phone rang. "Hello," he said, raising it to his ear.

"How long?" Ryan simply asked. Junior understood. They were the only two words he needed to hear.

"What do you need?" Junior replied.

"I need three," Ryan told him.

"Half an hour," Junior said.

"Okay." Ryan hung up. He looked at Amy with a boyish smile. She loved his smile, an attribute that made her fall in love with him. She adored men who made her laugh and feel comfortable enough to relax. She believed they were a perfect fit, like blizzard-cold hands in the warmth of mittens.

She glanced at him curiously. "What was that all about?"

"Relax, baby, I have a surprise for you," he said. He walked to the kitchen, searching for paraphernalia. He went to the refrigerator and opened the door. He took out a box of Arm & Hammer baking soda and placed it on the wooden counter next to the stainless-steel sink. He opened the cabinet beside the sink and grabbed an average-size plate. He picked up an old stiff sponge hidden under the sink, soaked it with water, and placed it in the freezer. Amy stood, confused, at the kitchen door, watching him inquisitively.

Ryan stored empty plastic Pepsi bottles in the recycle bin by the cellar door. He walked over to the blue bin labeled RECYCLABLE and snatched a Pepsi bottle. He took the scissors from his knife-holder, a roll of black electrical tape from the toolbox on the floor, a small piece of Reynolds Wrap tinfoil, and a safety pin from the kitchen drawer. He placed the items on a white plate and carried them to the maple coffee table in the living room. Amy followed close behind, watching with a piercing stare.

Using all the items he gathered, he crafted a homemade pipe and finished it off by pushing a straw through the hole on the side of the bottle.

Retching and gagging, he brought the pipe into the bedroom. He stood it on the bureau and ran to the bathroom to shit his brains out.

Amy ran after him. "Are you okay, Ryan? Are you sick?" she asked, with concern in her tone. She had not seen him this way before. Her mind wandered from food poisoning to water impurity from St. Maarten.

"No. No. I'm fine. It's just what happens before," he explained as he gagged. "You'll see later."

They left the bathroom and returned to the living room. Taking comfortable seats on the marshmallow-colored sofa, they watched an unprecedented Red Sox hammer the Yankees.

A rapid knock at the apartment door quickly sprung Ryan to his feet like a demon from hell. He picked up the white plate from the coffee table and placed it on the kitchen counter. He moved with reservation to the door and peeked through the Venetian blind. Seeing Junior, he cautiously opened the door.

"Hey Junior, how are you?" he asked, grinning from ear to ear with excitement. A hit from the pipe was only moments away.

Junior glided into a vast modern kitchen Ryan had painted coffee-brown before his wedding. Amy had decorated the walls with wicker-baskets, needlepoints she had spent hours creating, and cream-colored lace curtains on the two windows facing a well-spruced back yard. She loved decorating, and her knack for colors was a pleasure for anyone's eyes.

"Hello, Ry, what's up? I haven't seen you in a while," Junior said with a smile and a mouthful of bleached-white teeth. He turned and closed the door behind him, glancing out the window to make sure no prying eyes were there. Ryan locked the door and peeked through the blind. They sat together at the big butcherblock table that stood on a multi-colored Oriental rug in the center of the kitchen.

"Amy, come here," Ryan called. "I want you to meet Junior."

Amy got up from her comfort zone on the sofa and headed to the kitchen. Her eyes transfixed on Junior, a man of about twenty-five glowing from a stunning dark-brown complexion and African features. He wore meticulously pressed and fitted clothing, as though he had just stepped off a page of *Gentlemen's Quarterly*. Her smile spread from cheek to cheek as she stared at his chocolate eyes and thick, dark lashes.

"Amy, this is Junior," Ryan said.

"Hello, Junior, it is very nice to meet you," she remarked with a wide smile, deciding to like him before he ever opened his mouth.

He stood, staring back at her. He approached her with an outstretched hand, hoping she would reciprocate. She approached him with a smile and offered her finger-thin hand in approval. As Junior returned to his seat, Amy sat down, comfortably placing one foot under her buttocks.

Ryan placed one hundred twenty dollars in twenties from their wedding purse onto the table. Junior opened his plump mouth wide and relinquished four small, tightly knotted Baggies of white powder. He stood, slipped the twenties in his backside pocket, and walked to the door.

"Thanks Junior, I'll call you again soon." Ryan reminded him with a firm masculine handshake.

Amy smiled, and with a nod of her head she said, "Goodbye." Ryan closed and locked the door, once again peeking out the Venetian blind. He walked to the kitchen sink, placed the four small packages on the round white plate, and lifted a tablespoon from the utensil drawer. He reached for the scissors and cut open two of the Baggies.

Amy stood beside him, apprehensive, and watched him keenly. "After all the months of dating, I never realized you snorted lines," she said. "Why didn't you tell me?"

"Yeah, I have since high school, but that's not what'll happen tonight," he said. "I have something special planned, and that's why I never said anything."

Ryan nudged her arm with his elbow. "Stop bird-dogging me and sit on the couch," he said in an agitated voice. "I have to get this ready," He hated it when she stood over his shoulder as he tried to focus on something demanding. "I'll be done in a few minutes. Now get out of here and let me do this."

Amy brandished her head at his tone. With a stamp of her feet she turned, left the kitchen, and sat on the couch in silence.

Ryan finished his project and floated through the living room, humming a Frank Sinatra tune. The only stitch of clothing on his sleek body was the tattered shorts he wore only around the house. Amy's erotic juices started to flow in her fluffy center, wetting her black lace panties. At thirty, Ryan looked five years younger, and she reveled in his broad shoulders, hairy chest and gorgeous physique. He stood six feet tall and strutted gracefully through the room, like John Travolta in *Saturday Night Fever.*

He reached the bureau in the bedroom. "Okay, Amy, I'm ready. Come here," he shouted with a twinge of excitement in his voice.

Amy jumped up from the couch and sprinted to the bedroom with a sense of piqued curiosity. She noticed the round plate with an average hard rock of glossy white. Ryan stood beside it, half-naked. "You're so sexy," she told him with a longing in her throat.

"Yeah, yeah," he said, dismissing her and anxious to show her the surprise he had in mind. "Have you ever tried smoking coke?" he asked curiously while staring at her through bedroom eyes.

"No. Is that what this is?" she asked with a peculiar look. She had snorted cocaine but had no idea about smoking crack. She stood beside him, wiping her sweaty hands on her clothes.

"Yes, and believe when I say there is no high like it, and I know you'll love it." Ryan held the pipe in his left hand and the Bic lighter in his right. "I'll hold the pipe for you. You have to breathe in deeply and let it out. Suck on the straw and inhale like a cigarette, but hold the smoke in for as long as you can."

He stood beside her and lighted the white rock resting in the bowl of the pipe. She sucked on the straw as if it were a cigarette. He rubbed his lips with his forefinger, eager for his hit. As he stroked the palm of his hand through his blond locks, he gaped at Amy with lust and excitement. She inhaled and exhaled the smoke. He watched every crinkle of her face as she enjoyed her first hit of crack.

Unable to resist her body's natural reflexes, she coughed and gagged hard, expelling all of the smoke at once. "I don't think I like this," she snapped. "What's so great about this?" She coughed once more in Ryan's face.

He laughed so hard it made him choke. "Okay, try one more time, and this time don't suck in as hard," he said. "Take a small puff this time."

"No. I don't think I want to do this again. I'm not sure I like this, Ryan."

"Come on, baby. Just once more. Believe me; you're going to love it once you get it right. Go on now, once more."

She picked up the pipe. She inhaled deeply and exhaled slowly. She placed her mouth around the straw and sucked in slowly once again as Ryan clicked the lighter and held it to the top of the pipe. She held the circle of smoke in her lungs for a long time and exhaled again, more slowly this time. "That was much better," she told him.

Suddenly, a commanding euphoria overcame her total existence. Her head swooned as a fleeting rush overtook her body. She developed what some call the open-mouthed dead stare. Her muscles became alert, and her face went numb. Her tongue deadened as she submitted herself to the devil for the first time.

"This is great!" she exclaimed with delirium. "Oh, my God, Ryan, it is amazing and unbelievable! What an awesome feeling! Hurry, give me another hit!" She recognized in an instant the difference between sniffing and smoking coke. She doubted she would ever snort again.

He laughed at her once again. "No, it's my turn now," he said with a hurried look of anticipation. He held the pipe in front of his face, inhaled, exhaled, and took a long draw on the straw, holding in the smoke until he no longer breathed. It took him several minutes to expel the devil's breath as Amy stood, gazing at him, feeling her nerve endings twitch for another puff.

She drew on the straw once more as Ryan lighted the pipe for her and duplicated his hit procedure. After a few moments, she blew out the smoke, but with a different reaction. She did not feel her head swoon. She did not become mesmerized in the same manner. She stared blankly into space, and the real world disappeared. She wanted the same sensation as the first experience.

Ryan failed to explain to her that the "the chase was on" and would continue for another fifteen years. She did not know that being a crack addict would cause her unconsciously to buy and smoke more of the stuff, always seeking to relive the sensation of her first exhilarating hit.

They repeated their hit-sharing sequence a few more times. After the third or fourth, Ryan removed his shorts, exposing his manhood. He leaned in against her, grabbed the bottom of her Red Sox T-shirt, and pulled it over her head in a quick swoop. The shirt slipped to the floor. With his bold hands and smooth fingers he reached behind her and unfastened her bra, slid it down her delicate shoulders and exposed her full, plump breasts. He cupped them in his satin soft hands, squeezing and fondling them ever so hard, but gently. He leaned over and licked each nipple. He parted his lips and sucked each breast. Her nipples responded, hard and immediate. She moaned in ecstasy. She slipped out of her shorts and panties, kicking them aside with her right foot.

Ryan stared wantonly down at her pubic hair, as if he were a mythical Greek god. He knelt down and lightly blew on the tiny ginger hairs as she soared with pleasure.

"Spread your legs," he told her. She did as he commanded. He bent over and covered every inch of her sensual being with his manipulative tongue. She groaned and whimpered in delight.

"Lay on the bed," he instructed her, a wanting deep from within his throat. She lay on the king-size bed, and he spread her legs open. "I'm going to take you and take you hard. Ready?" he asked in a seductive accent.

"Oh, yes, please," she begged him.

He moved his first two fingers to her clit and rubbed hard, sliding them deeper into her creamy center. Her quivering lips and gasps for air turned him on. "Shall I finish you off?" he whispered in her ear.

"Yes, oh, God, please," she moaned in rapid

gasping breaths. He kept rubbing, and blew on her curly peach fuzz as she came ferociously all over his fingertips. "Oh, my God, this is the best orgasm ever."

"Good, I'm glad you got off. It was fun. Now get up so we can do another hit."

Ryan and Amy took two more hits of crack. The high sexually excited him. "Kneel on the floor," he told her. She grabbed a pillow from the bed, placed it down in front of Ryan's feet, and knelt down on it. She placed her hand on his cock and stroked gently, faster and faster. She bent over and placed it in her mouth, sucking hard and gently nibbling on the tip. With several strokes of her mouth and lips he exploded in orgasm.

Their routine of sharing hits and sexually pleasing each other lasted into the early morning hours. Amy scheduled her vacation time to last through the weekend, and now she smiled with delight not to have to return to work until Monday. She was ready to party all night. It would be Sunday in a few minutes, and she knew she could sleep late.

The next afternoon, Amy woke up next to Ryan. She found him snoring on his side of the bed. She lifted her head from the satin covered pillow and almost fainted. As she sat up, her stomach roared like a black panther. She felt like absolute shit. When her feet hit the floor, she swayed from a mental cloudiness filling her head and turning her stomach to sour milk.

She slithered out of the matching satin sheets and hobbled to the kitchen, where she loaded the automatic coffee maker. "I need a drink instead of a cup of coffee, or maybe just another hit off the pipe," she whispered to herself, but settled for coffee.

Ryan rose shortly after Amy and headed for the kitchen. "Hey, baby. Good morning," he told her as he bent over and kissed her. "Now, how did you like last night? Did you have fun?" he asked in a tone laced with sexual canniness.

She smiled at him and kissed him back. "Yes, but I would have appreciated knowing I would feel like shit. I do not like feeling this way. What can I do to feel better?" she remarked with a raspy throat from the pipe. She would do anything to rid herself of the crack hangover.

"Let's get another package," he said cunningly. "It will fix you right up. We have extra money from the wedding." They had four thousand dollars in wedding gifts, and it would buy countless packages.

Amy, however, had other plans for the money, and crack was not one of them. "I don't think so," she said. "Not yet, anyway. Let me drink my coffee." She sat at the same butcher block table where the night before money and coke had exchanged hands. She wondered what might happen to her, and if she was doing the right thing. She dismissed the thought quickly and began to prepare breakfast.

Ryan entered the bathroom off the kitchen for a shower and a song. He loved to sing around the house. He sang well enough to pursue a music career, but getting high had replaced his ambitions.

After dressing in sweats and a T-shirt, they ate a late breakfast of bacon and eggs. Amy sipped her hot coffee, waiting for her head to clear, which did not happen until late Sunday afternoon as she gathered her clothes for work. She returned to the couch and sat next to Ryan.

"So when did you start smoking coke?" she asked, looking at him inquisitively.

"I told you yesterday," he responded, slightly agitated. "I started after high school. Some of my friends turned me on, and the rest is history."

"After all this time, you never got caught?" she inquired, eager for more details.

"No, but I've been in some scary situations. I remember one time when I worked with my friend Kevin. He was a mason, and he got me a landscaping job. One Friday, after a ball-breaking day of work, he asked me to hang out for a while and have a couple of beers. We started talking about coke, and he wanted to get high. Around nine o'clock, I suggested we get a quarter-ounce. He told me his guy was better, and we headed to the Ashmont station in Dorchester."

"Oh, boy, this can't be a pleasant story—it's such a bad section of town," Amy remarked. Like almost any large city in America, Boston has its share of wealth and underprivileged. The wealthy side of Beacon Hill lies to the north. Dorchester and the surrounding towns are seven minutes to the south. Amy knew both areas and made it a point to stay clear of undesirable sections, especially in the late hours of the evening. She understood Ryan's hesitation.

"Yeah, it's bad," he said, continuing his story

with a shaky uneasiness in his voice. "We stopped in front of a rundown crack house. Kevin told me to wait in the car, and he would be out in a few minutes. I have dealt with Dominicans, Mexicans, Afro-Americans, and Puerto Rican dealers, but this section of Boston catered to Afro-Americans. I stood out like a zit on the end of your nose. I waited in the car for half an hour watching dudes pass by and stare at me through the windshield. They knew I was on their turf, for one thing. I really started to get pissed off when Kevin finally opened the passenger side door. That's when I said, 'What the fuck, are you out of your mind leaving me out here all this time?' He just laughed and said, 'Sorry, man, I was doing a couple of whacks.' I screamed at him, 'You're a fucking nut. You got me sitting here, sticking out like a sore thumb.' Kevin looked at me and said, 'You think *this* is bad, last week I was in here getting high, and the next thing I know I hear a loud boom. Three dudes with guns kicked in the door. They robbed the place and ripped my gold chain off my neck. It was some crazy shit.' Then I yelled at him, 'You're fucking shitting me. You got me parked out here knowing all this. You're an asshole,' I told him. "Kevin didn't say another word and just started laughing again."

"Wow, it is amazing you did not get robbed, or worse," Amy responded. "Someone could have killed you."

"As you know, not all drug transactions go right. It is the reality of a true addict. No matter what the cost or danger, you don't give a fuck. The mindset is about one thing, and one thing only, regardless of the consequences. Getting high is all that matters."

Later that afternoon they watched the Minnesota Twins beat the Atlanta Braves in Game 7 of the World Series while the unmistakable sweet odor of homemade Italian sauce and spices emanated from the chicken Parmesan baking in the oven. The pleasant aroma filled the entire apartment. Amy's cooking skills, though limited, satisfied their taste buds, and she did her best. Halfway through the sixth inning, she carefully positioned the place mats, the dinnerware and the utensils on the kitchen table.

"Ryan, dinner is ready," she called to him as he relaxed and watched the end of the last inning.

"Okay, I'm coming. Sure smells good," he said as he pulled a chair from the table and sat down. Amy brought her chicken Parmesan casserole to the table, placed it on a hot plate, and sat down in her favorite chair.

"Didn't you forget something?" he suddenly asked, harshly.

"No, I don't think so. Why, what's missing?"

"I can't believe you're that stupid. Where the hell is the grated cheese?"

Amy could not believe her ears. It was the first time since meeting each other that he had spoke to her with such irreverence. "Where the hell is that coming from?" she asked seriously.

"What do you mean?" he retorted. "Don't you think it's stupid to serve an Italian dinner and not have everything on the table? What the hell is the matter with you?"

Amy slumped down shamefully in her chair. A hurtful sulk flooded her face, making her speechless. Peeved at his irritable tone, she ignored him as she grabbed the Romano cheese from the refrigerator and slammed it down on the table.

"So what do you think?" he suddenly asked her. "Should we get a few more packages?"

"No. I'm tired, and I need to go to bed early," she irritably responded. "The shit will keep me up all night."

Amy went to bed early. Ryan stayed up to watch *Animal House* with John Belushi on TV.

Heather McCarthy

THE EARLY MONTHS

The loud, annoying buzzer rang out at six the next morning. Amy reached for the off button, knocking the alarm clock off the nightstand. *Shit, now I have to get out of bed,* she thought. *Such an irritating thought.*

Once her feet touched the floor, she showered, applied her makeup painstakingly, and reached for the clothes she had left on a chair before she had gone to bed. She poured her coffee with cream, no sugar, from the automatic coffeemaker. She gulped a few more sips of coffee, grabbed her identification badge and car keys from the wall hanger next to the door, and left for work, locking the apartment door behind her. Ryan lay in bed, snoring as loud as a bullhorn.

Amy began a career in hotel management and secured a position at the Presidential Hotel two days after graduating from college. She loved what she did for work, and her salary was more competitive when she compared it to other new graduates. She endured a long, exhausting day at work preparing schedules, dealing with irritating guests, and meeting with uncooperative co-workers, which provoked her to travel back roads to arrive home sooner than usual.

She opened the door to her apartment, and the smell of cocaine cooking alerted her that Ryan had returned home from his appointment with a landscaping client. He had established a partnership in a landscaping business with his brother-in-law before he married. He made a decent living and spent almost all of his days drumming up new clients.

As she walked through the doorway, Ryan stood at the stove and cooked the coke-filled spoon over the gas burner. The used pipe from two nights earlier rested on the kitchen table. The television screen flashed details and updates on the Rodney King trial. The jury found the four police officers guilty of civil right violations, and the newspapers carried the stories of numerous reactionary riots all over the country.

"Hey, baby, I figured you would be too tired to cook dinner, so I got something to pep us up," Ryan said.

"What, no dinner?" said Amy with a revolting smile and a rumble in her stomach from hunger pains.

"Yeah, I got a pizza. It's in the microwave," he hurriedly told her. "Change your clothes, have a slice of pizza, and by the time you finish eating, I'll be done."

"You know I had such a shitty day, it sounds like a good idea," she said. "I'll go get changed."

As she undressed, her body began to shake, and her head told her she needed a hit.

She returned ten minutes later, clad in pink baby-doll pajamas. She walked over to the kitchen counter, opened the microwave, and grabbed the platter with the three slices of lukewarm pepperoni pizza. She sat at the table, munching on the pizza and watching Ryan meticulously as he turned the white powder to an average-size hard rock. She heard a light "ting" sound as the rock fell from the spoon to her grandmother's Currier & Ives plate. Amy appropriately named it "the coke plate."

Ryan turned to Amy with a familiar and incredible boyish smile. "If you're finished eating, I'm all set," he said, leaving the kitchen toward the bedroom. Reaching the living-room threshold, he turned and ordered her, "When you're ready, bring me a bottle of water and hurry up. I want a *whack*."

That was a slang term for a hit off the pipe, and Amy had never heard the word before that day. Over time, she grew accustomed to the expression.

She placed her palms on the edge of the table and stood, pushing the chair out from behind her and hurling the pizza platter into the sink with a clang. She walked angrily to the refrigerator and, with an exasperating sigh, mumbled under her breath, "Screw him." She opened the new GE refrigerator—a wedding present from her parents—and reached for a bottle of Poland Spring water. She closed the door, and as she turned for the bedroom she began to gag and wretch as Ryan had done when he knew Junior was about to deliver a package.

When she entered the bedroom, her mouth opened slightly in surprise. Ryan stood naked in front of the bureau with the pipe in his left hand and a lighter in his right. He had her hit ready. She sucked on the straw, and the memories of irritating individuals at work and the stress of a long hard day instantly disappeared, but she needed another hit to achieve the feeling from the first day. Ryan sucked on the pipe and savored his hit as they passed the pipe back and forth for hours. Amy smoked hit after hit, trying to reach the exemplary sensation of her first one, but nothing compared with it.

She stripped off her baby doll pajamas, and Ryan's erotic appetite surged. He caressed her supple hair and grabbed her hard from behind her neck. He bent down and pressed his lips softly against hers as her body quivered. Ryan drew back his lips from hers. He moved his lips along her round face and long neck, sliding his mouth down to her copious breasts. He placed one breast in his mouth, sucking softly as he fondled and squeezed the other with his hand. He sucked the other breast until her nipple hardened. With his lips he followed her soft skin along her breastbone and down her stomach to her navel, pushing his tongue in and out until she moaned. He pushed her down hard on the bed. He slipped his hand between her thighs and firmly spread her legs open. He pressed two fingers over her clit and manipulated her vagina with his thumb until she groaned in ecstasy.

Amy cried out in pleasure. Exhausted from her orgasm, she lay still until her body shuddered for another hit. She rose from the bed, and Ryan set up the pipe for her next hit. She smoked hers and returned the pipe to him. She returned to the bed, and he wanted her again. He mounted her, spread her legs with his, and entered her moist, tight vagina. He thrust in and out slowly. He repeated his thrusts, but never achieved an orgasm, because the crack had turned him limp and soft.

They returned to the bedroom and stood in front of the mirror for another hit. The crack urge overcame their appetite for sex, and they enjoyed the next couple of hours just alternating hits.

Amy moved to the living room and played solitaire to quiet her nerves. The quick turning of cards calmed her while the effects of the crack-high diminished. She returned to the bedroom every ten minutes to grab a hit while Ryan watched porn videos in the bedroom.

Around two in the morning, they finished the crack rock, but still wanted more. Too much time passed, and Ryan knew Junior would not venture out so late. Ryan and Amy began to "Jones," a familiar term used to reflect an intense desire for another hit, but unable to satisfy the compelling urge. Their bodies grew antsy, rigid, and wet with sweat. It took alcohol or a joint to ease the mounting anxiety.

Amy knew that because of the late hour she would never make it to work on time. She headed to the kitchen to prepare a libation of Captain Morgan rum and Diet Coke to relax and control her withdrawal symptoms. She rubbed her eyes and took a seat in the La-Z-Boy recliner next to the telephone. She lifted the handset with a wobbly hand and dialed.

A voice sprang to life, "Good morning, Presidential Hotel. This is the reservation's desk. May I help you?"

Amy recognized the voice immediately. "Jill, this is Amy." Jill, a cute young blonde-haired woman with the body of Meg Ryan, worked the night shift. Amy had known her for five years, and they became close friends. Before she met Ryan, Amy and Jill used to barhop on weekends. At the time neither of them found any serious relationships. Jill remained single and looking while Amy met Ryan. Amy and Ryan fixed her up with a few of his friends, but Jill never found anyone worthwhile.

"Oh, hi, Amy, What's up?" answered the sweet voice of a young woman still in her prime.

"I'm sorry, but I'm feeling really lousy and I won't be coming to work this morning," Amy explained with an anguished crinkle of her mouth and a guilt-torn face. It had been over a year since she called in sick. Before she started smoking crack, she had been as trustworthy as the rising moon and the setting sun.

"Okay, no problem. I'll let the day manager know, and I hope you feel better."

"Thank you Jill. See you tomorrow. Goodbye." Amy hung up the handset, turned on the television, and sipped her drink of rum and coke, allowing her to feel sleepy. She finally rolled into bed around six.

She woke up at two in the afternoon, inhaling the sweet aroma of fresh-cut grass and the sound of a neighbor's droning lawn mower. The dead leaves cluttered the sidewalks, and the temperatures were still warm enough to cut the grass once more before the snow fell. Ryan had already left for work. The emptiness in the apartment filled her pale face with a sense of loss and a sad droop, though she did not understand the reason.

The next three days were crack-free, but Friday and party time arrived fast. Ryan and Amy bought six packages and spent three hundred sixty dollars over the weekend. They began to develop an undeniable routine. Monday morning, Amy went to work with a crack hangover and a sour feeling in her stomach, which lasted all day.

Their schedule remained etched in stone. Over the next few weeks, their weekly routine included getting high on weekends and paydays. They blew five hundred a week and, after depleting their wedding purse, began using their paychecks to support their habit. More than half of their paychecks paid for packages, but Amy was still conscientious enough to pay the bills with the leftovers—though the bank called about bounced checks, the electric and gas companies threatened to terminate service, and they forgot to make a car payment.

On Thanksgiving Day, Ryan dialed Junior. It would be a long weekend, which meant four nights to party. Ryan let the phone ring ten times without any answer. After jonesing for an hour, he called his friend Dennis.

"Hello," the earpiece snapped.

"Hey, Dennis, it's Ryan. How are you?"

"Good, man. What's up?"

"I'm trying to score, and my guy is out of town.

Do you have anyone?"

"Yeah, hold on."

Ryan stared blankly at the wall as he heard the tap from the receiver, and the phone went silent.

A minute later, Dennis returned to the phone. "Got his number, but you need to come here, because he doesn't know you," Dennis said. "He won't do business with you unless I introduce you."

"That's cool," said Ryan. "How long?"

"Give me half an hour."

"Okay. Should I call you back, or will you call me."

"I'll call you," Dennis told him, and the phone went dead.

Ryan and Amy hooked up with Dennis forty-five minutes later. Dennis and his wife rented a home within walking distance from their apartment. Amy followed Ryan up the two concrete steps as he rang the doorbell.

The door opened, and a handsome dirty-blonde-haired man of about thirty stood in the doorway. He appeared taller and much thinner than Ryan did, and with his shirt off, Amy's mouth watered at the muscular tanned biceps of a man who worked in construction. She loved Ryan, but had no regrets about admiring the good looks of other men.

"Hey, man, how the hell are you? Haven't seen you for a while," Dennis said with a smile and inviting tone.

"Hey, Den. Yeah, I know I got married a few months ago, and I've really been busy with the business." Ryan turned slightly and smiled at Amy.

"This is my wife, Amy. Say hello to Dennis," he told her.

Noticing how handsome Dennis was as he stood in the doorway, she looked in his honey-brown eyes and smiled. "Hi Dennis, it is a pleasure to meet you."

Ryan and Amy followed Dennis into the living room, from where she saw a lanky blonde-haired woman with a strikingly eye-catching face seating in the distance at the kitchen table.

"Amy, this is my wife, Linda," Dennis said as he turned and approached his gorgeous wife. Amy smiled. Linda rose swiftly from her chair and approached Amy gracefully, as if strolling down a fashion-show catwalk. Amy opened her eyes wide and parted her lips slightly in awe of the woman's beauty.

Linda approached Amy with outstretched arms and hugged her tightly. "Hi, so nice to meet you. We didn't know Ryan got married. How nice. Come in, sit down," she said, pointing to a large living room and a black leather couch.

Linda weighed about a hundred pounds and had large blue eyes and dilated pupils. Her face appeared hollow, and she seemed to shake with agitation. She spoke fast, but with a polite tone.

The four of them took seats in the living room. While discussing life as newlyweds and how many packages they needed, a knock resounded at the door. Dennis jumped from his seat, approached the door cautiously, and peeked through the peephole. Secure from neighbors' prying eyes, he opened the door, and a man entered.

A short, nicely dressed Jamaican man with dreadlocks and features of a boy no older than eighteen stood in the doorway. "Hey, Nokie. Come on in," Dennis commanded, rushing his visitor through the entryway.

"Thanks, man," Nokie replied urgently, closing the door behind him. Noticing Ryan, he nervously jerked his chin up at him and asked, "Who is he?"

"This is my good friend Ryan, and that's his wife Amy." Dennis quickly turned and glanced at Ryan. "I've been cool, not to worry."

Ryan rose from his seat and approached Nokie with his outstretched hand. "Hey, man. I'm Ryan," he said, towering over the little man and making him more uncomfortable.

Nokie timidly shook Ryan's hand, turned to Dennis and asked, "So what do you need?"

"Give me six," Dennis quickly replied as he handed Nokie two hundred forty dollars.

Nokie slipped his right hand inside the waist of his pants and down into his ball-bag. From under his balls, he produced a Ziploc bag holding twenty or more packages. He took the money from Dennis, opened the bag, and handed him six packages.

"See you later man, and just so you know, I won't be around tomorrow." Nokie explained.

"That's cool, man, no problem," Dennis said as he opened the door and let Nokie out. He swiftly closed it behind him and looked at Ryan. "So do you want me to cook a couple, and we can do a few whacks?"

Ryan, hesitant about sharing, frowned, but shook

his head in agreement.

After the four of them got high on two of the packages, Ryan tilted his head in Amy's direction, suggesting they leave. They walked the short distance home, high as a giraffe's pussy.

As soon as they entered the apartment, Ryan approached the sink and cooked the two remaining packages. They partied alone until two in the morning.

They woke up Thanksgiving morning, lethargic and nauseous from their crack hangover. Ryan's sister Patti had planned a two o'clock dinner at her home, but Amy knew how impossible it was to attend. Ryan picked up his cell phone from the bedroom end table and dialed Patti.

"Hello, baby. Happy Thanksgiving," he said into the receiver.

"Hey Ryan," Patti replied. "You too, honey, Happy Thanksgiving. What's up?"

"Amy and I have a bug and we won't make dinner. Sorry, baby, we don't want to infect the whole house," he told her with a small shakiness in his voice from a hangover and an obvious lie.

"Oh, too bad, I'm sorry to hear you're ill. Okay, stay in bed and get better," she responded sincerely.

Patti resembled Ryan, with fair features and dirty-blond hair. Her face was round, and they shared the same icy-blue eyes. As Ryan's older sister, Patti had prepared holiday dinners ever since Amy had met her. Amy came from a dysfunctional family where a day did not go by without her brother making fun of her. Ryan's family, on the other hand, was as tight as woven Spandex. His family always spent holidays together and stood by each other regardless of the consequences, but they never knew Ryan was a crackhead. Amy held Patti in high regard as a homemaker, and her face collapsed in guilt. She knew it was impolite not to spend Thanksgiving dinner with Patti after all the work she had put forth. Ryan's mother was still alive, and he had one brother, Robert. It would be the first time he would miss a family holiday since his wedding.

On this first Thanksgiving since their marriage, Ryan and Amy celebrated alone with a ten-pound turkey, mashed potatoes, and gravy. The rest of the night they watched television and went to bed early. The next day they returned to work, and in the evening they were on the phone calling Junior for a package.

Ryan and Amy visited Dennis and Linda only on rare occasions, because it is common for addicts not to share their drugs. The weekends progressed with the same routine for the next several months, including paydays and a sick call on Friday. Amy started to suffer from migraines caused by calling in sick too much and feared she would jeopardize her work. But she ignored the problem until it smacked her in the face.

A month later, her boss called her into his office. An eerie feeling that it might not be good news overcame her. She frowned with remorse as she entered.

"Thanks for coming in this morning Amy. Please sit down," he told her. Her boss wore a ridiculous brown toupee to cover his balding scalp, and it shifted from side to side every time he scratched his head. His dark wire-rimmed glasses slid down his nose. He weighed two hundred eighty pounds and, with a height of about five feet, looked like Humpty Dumpty in the flesh. Amy pressed her lips together tightly to suppress her intense urge to laugh.

"Amy, you're such a good worker, and it pains me to say I must let you go," he told her. She narrowed her eyes and tightened her lips. At that instant, she lacked the art of speech for someone so articulate. Her boss glared at her.

"What?" she asked in disbelief, not comprehending the gravity of his words. "I do not believe it! How can you fire me just like that without any warning? I do not understand."

"Amy, I do not need to give you any warning. We have a strict attendance policy here at the Presidential Hotel, and I'm afraid you have exceeded it by three days. It is out of my hands. It is hotel policy. I must let you go. I'm sorry. I instructed payroll to cut you a check this morning, and it includes today's pay plus any vacation time you earned."

He rose from the brown leather chair behind his desk and handed her a white envelope containing her check. She took it reluctantly, rose from her seat, and angrily stomped to the office door, slamming it behind her as she left.

Breaking the speed limit, she arrived at her apartment at nine in the morning. She opened the door and threw her purse on the floor, igniting her wild Irish temper. She ripped her clothes off and headed for the shower. She stood under the hot, pulsating water, blubbering like a child.

She dried her hair, pulled her Boston Bruins T-shirt over her head, and slipped into a pair of Danskin sweats. She stretched out on the living room couch, watched soap operas, and mumbled to an empty room, "How appalling to lose a job. My God, what will Ryan say?"

Ryan arrived at two in the afternoon. "What are you still doing up?" he asked seriously, genuinely concerned for her well-being. "Are you sick? Why aren't you sleeping?"

"No, I got fired."

"What?" Ryan yelled in anger.

"I said I got fired! My asshole boss fired me for calling in sick!" she hollered at him. She had worked hard her whole life and had never lost a job until now. She had put in long hours, and covered weekends while her co-workers were off enjoying themselves. It was so unfair that her boss could fire her. She began to cry.

"What the fuck!" screamed Ryan. "You gotta be shitting me. How the fuck could you let it happen? *Fuck!* What are we supposed to do now? We can't pay the bills on my salary alone! Shit!"

"Relax," she said. "I'll go on unemployment, and with my qualifications it should not take long to find a job."

"Yeah, that's just great! We are already two months behind on the rent! We have to pay it before the landlord evicts us! The Internal Revenue Service is breathing down our necks, damn it!"

"Well, it is not *my* fault you blew through all our wedding money!"

"What the fuck do you mean? Like I did it all by myself, you didn't do any of it, did you? I'm the only one who got high, is that what you're trying to tell me? You're a good shit! Remember it takes two, sweetheart! Well, you better get on the phone first thing tomorrow and apply for unemployment!"

"Hey, asshole! Tomorrow is Saturday! I cannot call until Monday!" She smiled spitefully, knowing she achieved the upper hand. It pissed her off to think he blamed her.

"Whatever, you better be on the phone first thing Monday morning!" he shouted back at her.

She started to cry again and only replied, "Okay." For a couple that loved each other, the constant fighting and bickering began to split them like a finger-slice from a paper-cut.

"Now, I got paid today and I think it's a good idea to get a couple of packages," Ryan said suddenly. "It's not like you have to go back to work any time soon, and after the day you had, I think you need to get high."

Amy's soft face turned rigid as she stared at him in disbelief, but it did not take her long to agree with him. She needed a hit off the pipe.

Ryan made his usual call to Junior, but the cell phone kept ringing, "I'll call Dennis and get his guy," he said as he hung up and dialed Dennis.

"Hello!" Dennis answered gruffly, annoyed with Ryan for disturbing his "high."

"Hey, Dennis, how long?" Ryan asked. "Okay, man, see you in an hour." Turning and looking at Amy, he said, "We have an hour to eat. What's for dinner?"

"I'm so upset I didn't feel like cooking dinner. Shall we order out?" she asked curiously with a half-smile.

"What do you think about Chinese?"

"Sounds good to me," she said.

Ryan ordered spare ribs, chicken wings and fried rice, not worrying about the overdue bills, and ran out the door within the hour.

PROGRESSIONS

When Ryan and Amy arrived at Dennis's house, they found Nokie waiting on the couch. Ryan and Dennis split ten packages for three hundred dollars, because drug-dealers cut special deals for quantity. Nokie left, and the party began. Dennis walked to the stove and cooked three packages. Amy and Ryan followed him to the colonial kitchen and pulled a chair from the oak table.

"Can I get you guys a drink?" Linda politely asked as she opened the freezer for a tray of ice. Ryan and Amy agreed on vodka and cranberry juice. Linda strolled gracefully to a large kitchen cupboard, removed four glasses, and poured the drinks. Her slender fingers completely encircled the glasses as she placed them on the table.

She turned to Amy. "Would you like to see the house?"

"Yes I would love to," Amy replied, rising from her chair. She followed Linda out of the kitchen for a tour of the first floor, leaving the boys to cook the coke.

Several minutes later, the girls ascended the staircase to two bedrooms and a bathroom. The rooms were messy with unmade beds and cluttered laundry on the floor. Linda had decorated her home with a distinctive colonial motif of fiddle-back chairs with needlepoints and tapestries. Amy found it rather charming.

"I love your décor," she told her.

"Oh, thank you—my grandmother gave me the tapestries when we moved in, and most of the furniture belongs to our relatives," Linda explained with a bashful smile. "Dennis and I don't make enough money to afford them." Earlier that day, Ryan had enlightened Amy that Dennis and Linda smoked crack every night. Amy looked at the blemished furniture and the floors, which needed an extensive scrubbing.

Returning to the kitchen, the girls found the boys seated at a square table with beers and a fat crack rock ready for the pipe. The four of them passed the pipe back and forth among themselves for an hour, when suddenly the mood changed.

"Hey, Linda, are you NBA tonight?" Dennis inquired, displaying a pretentious smile.

Ryan smiled and glared at Amy. Noticing her bewildered expression, he explained, "NBA means No Bra Association—in other words, it means she's not wearing a bra."

"So this 'NBA thing' is common knowledge?" she asked, a bit perturbed. She had never heard the term before that night and did not want to seem foolish thinking Linda knew while she did not.

He laughed at her heartily. "Yeah, I would say most guys, and maybe a few women."

"I get the picture. It's just another one of your

favorite expressions, like that one about the beef. What is that again?"

Ryan laughed. "You mean Doctor O'Connor's two-ball beef compound. It cures everything from a headache to a hangnail." The group roared with laughter.

"Oh, Ryan," Amy spouted annoyingly. She turned in Linda's direction and said, "I hope you do not intend to answer his question, do you?"

Linda giggled. She pulled her blouse up and over her head, exposing her small, firm breasts and slightly extended nipples. Everyone howled.

Ryan glared at Amy. "Don't look at me," she exclaimed, wide-eyed with a crimson blush on her cheeks. Such ideas never entered her head, and she hoped they did not expect her to remove her blouse.

"Oh, come on, Amy, we're all friends here, and it's just between us. No one will ever know, and besides you have voluptuous breasts."

"No way, Jose, I can't do it." She lowered her head in embarrassment and stared at the glass of vodka and cranberry. She lifted it and took two large gulps of the concoction.

Ryan placed his hand on hers. "Come on, baby, it'll be fun," he said in a calming yet encouraging tone. Amy threw him a disgusted look and shook her head more than once to show her disapproval.

The three of them began to heckle her. "Come on, Amy, take off your shirt! Do it!"

She still refused, but once the pipe came around to her for another hit, Amy's body began to tingle with ecstasy from the crack. She pulled her shirt over her head. "Okay, now you two," she insisted, glaring at Ryan and Dennis. The boys smiled at her and removed their shirts.

"Let's go in the living room," Dennis suggested.

As they moved there, Dennis sat on the loveseat. Linda stood, facing him while Ryan and Amy took a seat on the leather couch. Linda slid out of her sweats, pulled down her black lace panties, and kicked them aside with her foot. Dennis ran his hands over Linda's buttocks, digging into her cushiony flesh. He squeezed them tightly and spread them apart to expose her crinkled pink crevice to watchful Ryan.

Ryan smiled lustfully and nodded his head in pleasure.

Dennis circled her ring with his forefinger and slowly probed in and out as she gasped for air in both pain and ecstasy. Placing a hand on her shoulder and another on her waist, he turned her around to face Ryan. As Ryan admired her breasts, Dennis nestled his fingers in her blond curly hairs and spread her moist lips as he massaged them until her juices flowed.

Ryan smiled at her full-firmed essence, and his cock expanded in throbbing jerks. He turned to Amy and unbuttoned her pants. Ryan slid her pants and panties off as she squirmed in harmony through his hands.

Dennis watched them attentively as he fondled Linda's backside, turning her around again to suck on her breasts one after the other. He grabbed her wrist, forcing her down on the loveseat as he shifted his body and mounted her.

Ryan and Amy gawked at them with pleasure as Dennis slid in and out of Linda's vagina. As the rhythm increased with each thrust, moans escaped Linda's mouth as her body responded, limp from the orgasm.

Meanwhile, Ryan moved his hands over Amy's legs, stroking her shapely calves and spreading her thighs open. He bent over her and tongued her clit. He softly blew on her curls and entered her vagina with his tongue. With fast and swift stimulation he satisfied her to orgasm as she groaned deeply with delight.

Amy sat up and noticed the watchful eyes of Dennis and Linda. Embarrassed with public foreplay, she spoke softly, "Let's do another hit."

"Sounds good to me," Ryan responded with excitement, leaping from the couch.

As Dennis rose from the loveseat and walked back to the kitchen table, Amy giggled as his penis bounced from side to side with each stride. "I'll get one ready." Linda followed behind him *au naturel.*

Ryan rose from the couch and offered his hand to Amy. As she grabbed it, he lifted her up and off the sofa in a quick swoop. They followed Linda to the kitchen table.

Ryan and Dennis slid back into their denim jeans. Neither of them was wearing underwear.

"Wait a minute," Amy said. "This isn't fair. Linda and I are in our birthday suits. What about you guys?"

The guys laughed under their breath and slipped

off their jeans. The four sat at the table naked, drinking, and laughing as they passed the pipe back and forth for another hour.

After a few more hits, Ryan turned to Amy. "Hey, baby, come over here," he told her in an erotic but commanding voice.

She rose from her seat, slowly approached Ryan and stood directly in front of him. "Kneel down, baby," he demanded. "Taste me. You know what I want."

Amy turned and glanced at Dennis and Linda. She noticed they had already assumed the same position. She turned back to Ryan, knelt down at his feet, and spread his legs wide. She snuggled her shoulders in between his thighs and placed his soft penis in her mouth. His cock burst forth, pulsing blood and desire into an erection, but he quickly became soft and limp. Obsessed with smoking another hit, it became impossible for him to get hard enough to reach an orgasm.

"Sorry, baby, I don't think I can come," he explained. "Just keep sucking for a while." Amy engulfed his cock until her efforts became futile. The similar reaction plagued Dennis and Linda. The girls returned to their seats and passed the pipe around some more.

After another hour, Ryan rose from the table and announced, "It's two in the morning. I think it's time for us to leave. Hey, guys, thanks for everything, but we're outta here."

"Okay, guys, you're right. It's too late to call for more," Dennis declared. Ryan and Amy dressed and headed for the door, walking the short distance home, relieved they did not have to drive. When they reached the apartment, Ryan went to bed while Amy watched an old movie on TV and sipped another cocktail, trying to make it easier for her to fall asleep.

Saturday morning, Ryan and Amy woke up around noontime to a typical crack hangover and realized they had spent their paychecks. The cupboards were bare, so Ryan drove to the nearby Shaw's Supermarket. He bought a week's worth of groceries with his credit card and some smaller pocket items with a five-finger discount. He returned around two o'clock. Amy helped him put the groceries on the counter. Without saying anything, she checked each item against the list she gave him, and once everything checked out, she stored them in the kitchen cabinets. He had bought chicken and steaks for the weekend barbecue, ice cream for an evening snack, and plenty of vegetables.

After storing the groceries, she prepared dinner. Ryan and Amy ate in silence and vegged out in the living room watching television until Ryan picked up the telephone. "Hey, Junior, how long?" he asked. "Okay, see you in twenty." Ryan rose from his favorite La-Z-Boy recliner and lowered the window shades in the bedroom and kitchen.

"What the hell are you doing?" Amy screeched.

"Relax," he replied soothingly. "I took out a cash advance on my credit card."

"Oh, no, Ryan, why did you take out more money? It will be hard to pay them with no money coming in. What are we going to do?" she asked pensively. The last things she needed were more unpaid bills, but somehow he always found the money to get them by until payday. She sighed and tossed him a dirty look to show her disapproval.

"Don't worry about it. We will get by," he reassured her.

Twenty minutes later, Junior knocked at the door. Ryan peeked through the Venetian blind and opened the door halfway. "Hey, Junior. Where have you been? I've been calling you for days."

"Hey Ry, sorry man. I've been out of town. I took a drive to New York to up my supply. What do you need?"

"Little short on cash this week, so just give me three." Ryan placed the cash on the table, and Junior replaced the money with three packages. Junior turned and left, closing the door behind him. Ryan and Amy got high again, this time to escape the memory of the mounting bills.

Regardless of the occasion, Ryan and Amy always made plans when they were crack-free. When they awoke from a cocaine-induced stupor, the plans changed, causing them to bail on friends and family. With any addiction comes excuse after excuse. Getting high occupied all of their free time, and the enjoyment of family and friends became non-existent. They spent nights alone getting high and their days in bed recovering from hangovers.

On the following Saturday afternoon, as Ryan watched the Miami Hurricanes defeat Boston College 18 to 7, a blank stare flooded his face. He sprang from the couch as though he was in a hurry. He turned to Amy. "I just thought of something. I'll be right back."

"Where are you going?" she inquired, surprised to see him grab his car keys. "I thought you wanted to watch the next game?"

"Chill out! I have an idea. I'll be back in an hour." He took his windbreaker and left without another word. She wondered where he was going. She knew he did whatever he wanted, and once he decided on something, it was useless to try to change his mind. Amy spent the time watching an old Turner Classic movie.

It was a little after dinnertime when he returned. "Where the hell have you been?" she asked, looking furiously at him because the pot roast she had made for dinner had dried out.

Ryan walked past her with a smile and entered the living room. He sensed her eyes staring at him as she followed him, waiting for a response. "Well, where were you?" she asked again.

"I went to see my sister. I told her I needed a hundred dollars to pay the electric bill."

Her mouth fell to her feet. "What?" she scowled. "Why did you do that? Did she give it to you?"

"Of course she did. She's my sister," he told her, wearing a grin from ear to ear. He watched her as she shook her head in disbelief. "Don't worry about it. I'll take care of it."

"Yeah, you'll take care of it all right, like everything else," she snapped, throwing him a disgusted look.

Without another word Amy turned her face from him and prepared the table for dinner. He cut the pot roast while she mashed the potatoes. Before he sat down to dinner, he called Junior.

Ryan and Amy finished dinner in silence, staring down at their plates. After Junior had left, they spent the rest of the night getting high. With the exception of work and grocery shopping, they never seemed to leave the apartment. The daily crack-induced irritability blossomed into sharp tongues and cutting glances.

Monday morning came. Ryan showered and left for work while Amy spent the entire morning on the telephone with the unemployment office. By the end of the conversation, the agent informed her she would receive her first check in five weeks. "Such a long time to wait," she told the four walls in the empty apartment.

The next day Amy bought a newspaper and searched the Internet for employment, but found nothing. *What will happen if I'm unable to find a job?* she asked herself. *I can ask my father.* She thought twice and came up with "no," even though her father would give her anything. He had told her so many times in the past. She did not want to let him know she was in trouble. It was by far too embarrassing.

The bills were three months behind, and the money they earned continued to go down the toilet—or, in this case, to the devil.

On an arctic morning in January, as Ryan and Amy cuddled under the down comforter, she heard an unusual sound. It was a sound of nonexistence. She rose from the bed and moved to the kitchen for her daily ritual of morning coffee when she realized the coffeemaker did not work. She fiddled with the buttons, looked at the wall outlet, and jiggled the cord. She still heard nothing. She reached for the light over the kitchen sink and groped for the wall switch. "Damn it, where the hell is the switch?" she asked herself. She found it and flicked it to the on position—still no light. The only light in the kitchen came from the early morning sun scattering through a narrow window above the sink. She noticed all of the wall switches were in the on position and finally realized the strange sound was silence.

She hastily ran back to the bedroom and shook Ryan awake. He awoke, dazed and irritable.

"What the fuck is the matter?" he shouted as he rolled over and hugged his pillow once again.

Amy shook him hard once more and shouted, "The power is out!"

"Damn it, Amy, can't you fix it?" he growled at her.

"No, I do not know how! Please help me!"

He rose from the bed, grumbling and swearing, "What the fuck, Amy! I can't believe you got me up for this shit! It's freezing in here!" She had decided to lower the heat before she went to bed to save money. "Put the heat on!" he shouted. He fumbled through the kitchen drawer, searching for the fuse.

Amy walked to the thermostat on the wall. The temperature gauge was at fifty-eight. She turned the dial to raise the heat, but did not hear the usual clicking sound of the furnace. She returned to the kitchen and watched Ryan as he grabbed the flashlight on the small table next to the cellar door. He descended into the dank, dark bowels beneath the apartment.

"Okay, Amy, try the light again!" she heard him shout from somewhere deep in the cellar. "Does it come on?"

"No, nothing!" she yelled back. She listened intuitively while Ryan finished his inspection of the fuse box. He ascended the staircase, mumbling something about the neighbors.

"Did you look outside to see if any of the neighbors have power?" he asked her.

"No, but I can look. Hold on a minute." She spread the lace curtain covering the window and peeked out. "Yes the people across the street have their lights on, and the street lights are still on from last night," she remarked, somewhat confused.

"Well, it's simple! The electric company has shut us off."

"You've got to be kidding me! Now what will we do?" she asked in a troubled, shaky voice.

"You'll have to call them and find out how much we have to pay to get the electricity turned back on."

"How am I supposed to call when the phone doesn't work? It is electric, too, you know!" She was frustrated, and feeling helpless made the condition worse.

"Don't be so stupid, Amy! Use my cell phone, damn it!"

Amy crossed the kitchen floor in her bare feet to

the living room and clutched Ryan's cell phone from the coffee table. She telephoned the electric company. After an exhausting game of recordings and pressing numbers, she pressed the end key. Walking back to the kitchen she explained to Ryan, "They said we have to pay a minimum of a hundred dollars. I have no idea where we'll find the extra cash," she said, frightened, tears rolling down her cheeks.

He hugged her hard and rubbed her back with his strong, comforting hands. "Not to worry. We can hook up a multi-plug extension cord to the basement outlet through the cellar door. The landlord will never know, and I'll see if I can borrow some money from my mother. We will be okay, don't you worry." He gave her another hug.

A limited amount of power returned to the apartment, and Amy settled with relocating lamps to reach the extension cord.

Later during the day, Ryan visited his mother. He always counted on her for two gifts every year—a fifty-dollar birthday present and a hundred dollars at Christmastime—both of which Amy and he had blown on crack. His father had died several years before he met Amy, and his mother always had extra cash to hand over to her favorite son, who always found a way to soften her heart and her pocketbook. She handed him two hundred dollars.

Ryan threw a hundred on the bill and bought three packages with the remaining cash. The lights returned three days later.

"By the way, I forgot to tell you earlier that my

mother wants us to go to my niece's birthday party next Sunday," he told Amy. "I told her we would be there."

"Okay, that should not be a problem. It is not like I work weekends anymore," she said as she went to the kitchen to prepare lunch. As she grabbed the loaf of bread and a package of bologna, she reminded herself to find a job, any job. She hated being out of work and had already managed to deplete most of her savings. Living in debt increased her irritability and frustration with Ryan.

She searched the newspapers and the Internet daily. She mailed over thirty resumes. She interviewed for an assistant manager position at a big hotel in Boston, but the company required drug testing and her urine came back dirty. The company never called her back.

Finally, Ryan recommended a new approach. "Why not come to work for me in the office? I can use someone with your talent and good looks," he told her approvingly.

"Oh Ryan, do you think it is okay?"

"Sure, but I'll have to check with my brother-in-law first."

"I do not think it will be a problem—after all, he's your brother-in-law." Ryan laughed.

Overjoyed at having a job and money coming in the house, Amy left for work with Ryan on Monday morning. He hired her as his temporary office manager for less money, but she had no choice. She danced a jig in the living room to Michael Jackson's "Beat It."

The landscaping office consisted of a magnificent reception area and two smaller private offices for Ryan and his partner. It was the largest room she had ever worked in, and she welcomed the extra space. The money began to pour in again, and the parties intensified. Sunday evening came and went. They forgot about the birthday party and never remembered to call or show their faces at his sister's home.

Two weeks later, when Amy cashed her first paycheck, they celebrated with a night on the town. She wanted to enjoy her first paycheck on something other than a package, so she disregarded Ryan's attempts to buy one. They enjoyed a candlelight dinner at a cozy little Italian neighborhood restaurant. Amy seemed happy to enjoy an ordinary existence once again.

She glared at Ryan's chiseled features as they shimmered in the candlelight across the table. It was a wonderful night. A boyish smile emanated from his limber lips, and a dramatic lock of blond hair rested on his forehead inches from his blue eyes. He gently placed her hand in his and kissed the upper side of her hand. "I love you very much, Amy," he declared in a sincere, remorseful tone, as he had unwillingly caused her so much grief. Her face flushed a warm shade of pink, and love sizzled once again in her soul after such a long time. With a yearning and a glow on her face, she wanted to seduce him.

Ryan and Amy enjoyed a romantic walk home from the restaurant on an unseasonably warm February night while watching the stars glitter in the sky. It had been a long time, but as soon as they entered the bedroom, they made slow passionate love. For the first time in months, they appreciated a crack-free weekend.

* * *

Though she now worked for Ryan, Amy fervently searched for a higher-paying job. One day, as she sat at her desk in her usual routine of answering the phone, filing contracts and flipping through newspaper ads, a well-dressed stranger entered the office.

"Good morning," she said to him. "May I help you?"

"Good morning to you. Yes, I certainly hope so," the attractive man replied. He wore a gray silk Armani suit, and everything about him reeked of money. Amy's face turned a blushing pink.

"What can I do for you?" she inquired.

"Such a leading question, if I ever heard one." He was already fond of her and inclined to do anything she asked. He noticed every striking detail about her. He realized the woman seated at the desk deserved his attention.

She glanced down at her wedding-ringed hand, intent on deterring the man's advances. He looked at her ring finger and saw a matched set.

"Oh, I'm sorry," he said. "I did not realize you were married. What a shame such a beautiful woman such as yourself is taken." His face shined a relaxing smile and relieved her of any further advances. "I own a hotel with two hundred rooms in Milton, and I'm looking for a permanent landscaping business, and someone recommended you. Is there someone I can speak to?" he inquired.

"Yes. I'll get the owner for you. He can help you. That is interesting—a hotel. I have experience with hotels."

"Really?" he paused, as if riveted in thought. "How much experience do you have?"

"I have ten years' experience as a receptionist and five years as a front desk manager."

"I see. Are you by any chance looking to advance? The work I have in mind might be a little beneath your qualifications," he remarked with a coy smile.

"It is odd that you ask. I'm seeking employment in hotel management, but it is extremely difficult to find any momentous positions these days."

"It just so happens I'm looking for a night manager. My present manager quit to start his own motel somewhere in Dorchester. He left me downstream without a paddle. Would you be interested in working eleven at night to seven in the morning?"

She wiggled back and forth in her chair, trying to control her excitement. "Oh, I do not think I would mind the night shift, but it might take time to adjust to those hours. I think I may be interested." She paused for a moment, trying not to be too anxious. "Yes, I would be very interested."

The gentleman reached into the side pocket of his Armani suit and revealed his wallet. He opened it and handed her a business card. "My name is George Mills, and here is my card. Whenever you're ready, please give me a call, but do not wait too long. I cannot hold the position forever."

Amy took the card from his hand. "Thank you so much, and I promise I won't take very long to decide." She glanced at the card, placed it in her pocket, and offered Mr. Mills her outstretched hand, which he accepted in approval. "Now I'd better get the owner so you can inquire about some landscaping for your hotel," she told him. They laughed exuberantly, giving the impression they had known each other for years.

By Friday, Amy had gained a manager's position at the Milton Arms Hotel, making more money than at her previous job, and Ryan had purchased the landscape contract. It would be party-time once again. Ryan and Amy returned home for dinner and a night of celebration. He placed an order with Junior for three packages.

As they waited for Junior to arrive, the telephone jingled.

"Hello, Louie." Ryan knew the caller before he lifted the handset, thanks to the modern invention of Caller ID.

"Hey, Ry, what's up? I haven't seen you in a long time."

"I got married. Her name is Amy, and she's extremely smart and attractive." Ryan cocked his head in excitement. "You should come by the apartment and meet her."

Louie responded in a straightforward tone, "Yeah

that's the reason I'm calling. Is your guy still around?"

"How weird is that? I'm waiting for him now. You have to come right now, though." Ryan relayed directions to the apartment. "What do you want?"

"Get me three, and I'll be right over," Louie said, and the phone went dead.

Ryan turned to Amy. "It was Louie, a friend you haven't met," he told her. "He wants to party with us. He will be here soon, so you better get dressed, comb your hair, fix your face, and wear something pretty."

Amy washed the dinner dishes, took a shower, and dressed in a pair of gray sweats and a white T-shirt. She looked beautiful, no matter what she wore. She glanced in the mirror at her gaunt, haunted expression. *I have to paint my face,* she told the mirror. She removed her makeup case from the vanity and carefully applied eyeliner and mascara. She pinched her cheeks with her thumb and forefinger to a pinkish color. She left the bedroom and joined Ryan in the living room.

Within minutes came a knock at the door. Once again, and as regular as a bowel movement, Ryan peeked through the Venetian blind and opened the door. "Hey Louie! How the hell are you?" he inquired, rushing Louie through the door and promptly locking it behind him.

"Great! How have you been?"

"Good, can't complain. Come in and meet the wife." Ryan and Louie strolled slowly into the living room.

Amy rose from the couch and stepped forward. "It is very nice to meet you, Louie," she said, offering an outstretched hand.

"Likewise, but please call me Lou," he told her as he started to take her hand, but instead pulled her close to his chest and offered a hug.

Amy smiled cautiously and noticed he stood two inches shorter than she did. He wore tattered jeans and a Boston Celtics T-shirt that had a faded light green color from too many washes. He parted his hair in the middle, and obvious signs of premature graying made him look older than his years. His oval eyes gazed at her through a brown sparkle. She extended her hand and offered him a seat in the La-Z-Boy recliner. He accepted graciously, and as soon as he became comfortable, Junior knocked at the door.

Ryan bought six packages from Junior—three for himself, three for Lou. The three of them shared the packages and smoked crack until two in the morning when they depleted the product. Lou drank a Cape Codder to calm his nerves and promptly left when he finished. He had a wife at home who was oblivious to his drug practice, and he did not want to anger her. He always slipped into bed quietly without waking her, and she assumed he was out late with friends.

With two dealers and friends like Dennis, Linda, and Lou, their habit progressed rapidly. Ryan and Amy smoked crack four nights out of seven and spent close to six hundred dollars a week. The four walls of the apartment began to close in tightly around them.

HOLES

Monday morning, Ryan and Amy woke up early for her first day at the Milton Arms Hotel. He drove her to work and to his appointment with George Mills to canvass the grounds and acquire signatures on a landscape contract. He turned off Route 128 and headed up Route 28 toward Milton. After about a mile, he drove down a short, winding driveway. The car ascended a steep hill, surrounded by heavy woods and trees that shadowed the road in phantom-like figures. As he rounded the last curve, Amy barely saw the tips of the three turrets peak above the tall New England pines. Atop the Blue Hill Reservation stood a grand old Victorian mansion.

"Oh, my, she whispered breathlessly, as she gazed up at its stained-glass oriel windows. "I'm in love."

Ryan drove around the Quincy granite driveway and stopped directly in front of an ornately scrolled door with arched windows. He looked at Amy. "I hope so," he said to her. "You'll be spending half your time here."

They walked into a grand, high-ceilinged lobby

decorated in mahogany and walnut furnishings. Parallel to a huge bay window stood two floral sofas of mauve and coral with a cherry coffee table in the center. Beautiful oil paintings of earlier times in Milton hung on all four walls. They met Mr. Mills just inside the entryway.

"Good morning," he said, extending a hand to Ryan. He then turned and smiled at Amy. "You look extremely professional. I love the navy suit and conservative pumps. It brings out your hair color and striking eyes."

"Thank you," she said with a glowing smile. "I wanted to look my best, and I appreciate the compliment," she told him sincerely, glad in the knowledge that she had impressed him on her first day.

"You're very welcome. I'm sure you'll fit right in here, and I'm happy you accepted the position. Are you ready to get started?"

"Oh yes. I can't wait."

He looked back at Ryan. "Have a seat, Ryan, while I get Amy settled, and I'll be back to go over my plans for the grounds." Amy walked away with Mr. Mills, and Ryan sat in a plush sofa facing one of the large bay windows. He gazed out the window at the town of Milton below. It was an awesome sight.

Mr. Mills introduced Amy to the day manager, who started her with a five-week training program. He returned to Ryan and gave him the grand tour of the gardens. Meanwhile, Amy perused the impressive mansion with its grand piano and extravagant chandeliers. As she looked out of one of the upstairs windows, she saw Ryan shake Mr. Mill's hand and leave.

She enjoyed her first day on the job, and ended it by telling her new co-worker, "Thanks for all the help and I'll see you tomorrow."

She drove herself to work the next day, refreshed. Ryan arrived late the same afternoon and drove to Pizza Hut for a cheese pizza and a Caesar salad. Arriving home, he told his wife, "Let's celebrate my hefty contract and your new job with a couple of packages."

"I cannot risk screwing up this job, too!" she protested adamantly. "It's a once in a lifetime opportunity." She made a gasping breath. "Did you see that place? In my whole life I have never seen so many antiques and imported china in one place. My God, it was just beautiful."

"Yeah, it's okay, I guess, if you like that sort of stuff. I thought it was a bit gaudy."

"I like it, and I can't afford to get fired again." She hated herself for allowing it to happen at all. They went to bed at eight in the evening and rose the next morning, refreshed, as if crack cocaine had not existed.

Amy, proficient in business administration, learned the hotel policies and procedures in two short weeks. She worked closely with Mr. Mills, and he introduced her to a small staff of six employees, two handymen, a chef, and a security guard. At the end of the second week, Mr. Mills congratulated her on her considerable skill and learning ability. He was ready to place her on the night shift earlier than he expected.

George and Amy established an excellent rapport, and it became obvious to the casual onlooker that they possessed a deep admiration for one another from the beginning. She received her first paycheck the following Friday. "I'll see you Monday night at eleven to begin my first night shift," she reassured him.

He cackled heartily. "No, I don't think so. It will be too late for me," he told her. "Don't worry. I have the utmost confidence in your ability." He laughed once again. "I wouldn't be letting you start the shift alone if I thought otherwise." He smiled warmly at her and gave her a friendly hug.

On the way home, she stopped to pay half the balance on the utility bills, then went to Shaw's Supermarket to buy two rib-eye steaks with sweet potatoes for dinner. She arrived home shortly before sunset.

Ryan walked in the door ten minutes later, and within seconds headed for the telephone. "How long, man?" he asked. "Okay, thanks. See you in an hour." He knew Amy would not say anything after a week of hard work.

The Milton Arms hammered Amy physically and emotionally over the course of her training. The ache in her lower back and two Percocet proved it. She smiled at Ryan without hesitation to the idea of getting high. With the spring season upon them, Ryan grilled the steaks on the Charbroil gas grill and baked the potatoes in the oven. They ate dinner at sunset on the patio furniture. They waved and acknowledged the passing neighbors as they enjoyed a flash of average living. There seemed to be fewer days left when she felt normal.

Amy picked up the dishes with leftover food and carried them into the apartment. She scraped them into the wastebasket and washed the dishes. She returned to the porch to wipe off the patio table and sat, admiring the neighborhood.

Ryan and Amy relaxed with a glass of red Zinfandel and watched the sunset. As dusk approached, they moved into the apartment and closed all the curtains. Smoking crack was not something you wanted to broadcast to the neighbors.

After jonesing and waiting over an hour for Junior, Ryan telephoned him again. "Hey, man what's up? How much longer?" he asked irritably. "Okay brother, I need six, not four." He turned to Amy. "He'll be here in five."

While she showered, Junior dropped off six packages for two hundred dollars. Normally, one package is forty dollars, but if you bought six, Junior charged a C-note for every three. Ryan cooked two packages in a spoon over the gas flame while Amy stepped out of the shower. Starting with her toes, and slowly moving over the curves of her smooth leg, she dried herself with a towel, opened the bathroom door expelling the steam, and walked to the bedroom wearing only the towel. Ryan stood at the bureau, naked, gagging, and ready with the pipe and lighter in hand. Amy allowed her hair to dry naturally and dropped her towel. She stood naked in front of Ryan. He smiled at her naked form.

"Ready?" he asked her.

"Let's go," she told him, trying to control her gag reflexes. She sucked on the straw and handed the pipe back to Ryan.

Once the euphoria overtook her, she sat on the edge of the bed with a vacant glare similar to a deer caught in oncoming headlights. She waited and stared at the blank television screen until Ryan finished his hit. He stood still with a round open mouth staring blankly into space. They each took two more hits, and after a short lapse he returned to reality and guided her hand to his penis. Reluctantly, while enjoying her buzz, she began to stroke his cock up and down slowly. Ryan's concentration quickly shifted to another hit, and he pushed Amy's hand away.

They enjoyed a few more hits, but Ryan's inability to achieve a hard erection did not diminish his thirst for sex. It only drove him closer to a kinky side of pleasure. "Lay down on the bed." She did as he asked. "I want to try something different tonight." Amy glanced at him curiously. "Raise your hands above your head." Not knowing what to expect, she raised her arms. Ryan wrapped black satin ties around her wrists and tied them to the bedposts. He circled the bed, staring down at her, "Spread your legs apart." he demanded in a slow, sexy voice. She did as he instructed. "Spread them farther apart." With her legs spread two feet apart he attached the leg ties to her ankles and tied them to the bed frame, pulling them taut.

He stood naked at the end of the king-size bed,

glancing down at her vulnerable nude shape. He lay on the bed, crawling in-between her legs, and spread her short, curly locks with his tongue as he found her clit. He teased her with his sucking tongue, biting and licking in circular motions until he reached her slit. He forced his tongue inside her as her juices flowed. She groaned loudly with pleasure.

With a peculiar look she said, "No one ever tied me up before."

"You like being tied up, don't you?" he asked. She moaned again. "Tell me you like it."

"Oh yes, I do," she responded, feeling guilty for enjoying the vulnerability of being helplessly bound to the bed.

"Yes, you do what? Tell me. Say the words." He probed her with his clear eyes.

"I like being tied up."

"Yes, you're a good girl. Now I'll make you cum." He placed two fingers in her creamy opening and slowly stroked in and out until her lips began to quiver. She screamed in blissful excitement. "Yeah, baby, come for me!" he exclaimed.

She moved her hips in his rhythm and exploded on his fingers. He undid her ties and lay down beside her. She rested her head on his strapping chest as he softly brushed aside the wispy strands from her face. He stroked the back of her head, down the length of her hair to her back, and firmly squeezed her buttocks.

"What fun," he whispered in her ear. Ready for another hit?" he asked.

The passing of the pipe continued. In the early

morning hours, after the crack euphoria wore off, Amy prepared a Captain and Coke to calm the jitters caused by the effects of the "come down," a common term for the slow decline of the euphoric rush of the drug. She slid in bed next to Ryan, but it took her an hour to fall asleep.

They slept late Saturday morning and never left the apartment. After they watched television and ate an early supper, the telephone rang. "Hello," Ryan answered. "No problem. I'll call him now." Glancing at Amy he said, "It was Lou. He wants to drop by tonight."

"But we don't have any more money," she enlightened him.

"We have credit cards." He had no illusions about taking out another cash advance.

"No, Ryan!" she shouted. "Our credit cards are maxed out! We cannot get any more cash!"

"Okay, we'll let Lou pay for it, but you might have to show him your tits, though."

"I hope you're joking," she replied despairingly.

"Do you want to get high, or not?"

Shocked at such a suggestion, the muscles in her face dropped in sadness. Her eyes glazed over as though deep in thought. No words escaped her mouth.

"Well, do you, or don't you?" he asked her again, this time more firmly. He was willing to do anything to get high.

"Yes, but show him my tits? You're not serious, are you?" She shuddered to think of his callous attitude.

"Hey, you know what they say. Tits are for tots, and besides, Lou will love it. Your tits are fine. Why not show them off?"

"I don't think so. It would be too embarrassing."

Ryan dialed Junior, but the phone rang ten times, so he hung up and dialed Nokie, "How long?" he asked. "Okay, I need three." He turned to Amy. "He'll be here in twenty. Now, if you want to get high, we'll have to get Lou to pay, so think seriously about showing him your tits."

Amy stood rigid with contempt, but quickly relaxed her body, waiting for the moment to present itself.

Nokie and Lou arrived at the same time. Ryan, with his usual paranoia and routine of checking the windows, opened the door. Nokie entered first, followed by Lou.

Once inside, Ryan closed the door and turned to Lou. "Lou, I want you to meet Nokie." The men smiled at one another, and outstretched palms exchanged hands.

"Hey, Nokie, I'm broke. Can you 'cuff me' [slang for "pay me later"], at least until payday?" Ryan inquired warmly.

"Gee, man, I can't," Nokie explained regrettably.

Ryan turned to Lou. "Hey, Lou, what about you? I'll pay you Thursday."

Lou dipped into his wallet and produced another hundred dollars. "Yeah, no problem, but I have to have it Thursday." He handed Nokie the money. Nokie slipped his hand down his pants and under his ball bag. He pulled out a plastic baggie with six packages. Nokie left, and Ryan transformed the coke to crack.

Amy and Lou got acquainted while seated on the living-room couch. Lou worked as a plumber at a big hotel in downtown Boston. He maintained his own bank account and gave his wife money only when she asked him for it. His wife had no idea he smoked crack, and he kept it a well-guarded secret. Lou and Amy found they had a lot in common and became instant friends.

Ryan passed through the living room a short time later. He made his way to the bedroom. When he reached the doorway, he turned. "You guys ready?" he asked impatiently.

Amy and Lou rose from the couch and followed Ryan into the bedroom. He handed the pipe to Lou as he turned to Amy. "Since he paid for it, he can do the first hit."

"Sounds fair to me," she said with a frown, jonesing for a hit. She always smoked alone with Ryan and hated the idea of having to share.

Lou sucked on the pipe, holding in the smoke. His face turned from a soft shade of pink to a deep red. As he expelled the smoke, his eyes stared blankly at the wall in a euphoric daze, and his lips opened wide with the slightest of drool escaping from the right corner of his mouth. Amy wiggled anxiously while Lou tightened his grip around the pipe, unwilling to release it.

"Wait a minute," he told her. She sighed and glared at him with envy. She reached out to grab the pipe. Lou quickly turned away from her grasp, "One minute," he said again. He sucked one more time for a second hit.

"Come on, it's my turn now," she insisted, reaching for the pipe.

He finally handed her the pipe. She grabbed it. "What the fuck!" she blurted. She held the pipe and lit it. She had come far enough to know how to light her own hit. As she expelled the smoke, she passed the pipe to Ryan.

Once Ryan finished his hit, he slipped out of his sweatpants and stood naked in front of them. He nodded his head at Amy. "Take off your shirt and show Lou your tits," he insisted, a longing in his voice.

She stood obtrusively with her hands on her hips. She stomped out of the room and sat in a corner of the couch, sulking.

After Ryan and Lou enjoyed their hits, it soon became time for another. Ryan turned to Lou, "The only way to relax her enough to show us her tits is to get naked. Let's drop trou and be bare-assed when she comes back in the room." Ryan and Lou stripped down to their birthday suits.

"Amy, you're up," Ryan barked out to the living room, where she was playing numerous games of solitaire. Keeping busy eased the anxiety of the comedown.

As she entered the bedroom, she found Ryan and Lou naked. She turned bright red in the face and snapped, "What the fuck?"

"Relax, and just do a hit," Ryan pleaded.

She took her hit, and the exhilarated effects of

the crack aroused her, making her oblivious to her previous unwillingness to comply with her husband's suggestion. She peeled her shirt off and stood topless before them. Frozen in shock, she realized what she had done. It was not something she wished to admit, but she knew it was just the crack and laughed it off nervously. She took her second hit and promptly left the bedroom, allowing Ryan and Lou to take theirs.

Embarrassed she retreated to the kitchen and waited for the next hit while mixing a glass of rum and Coke to soothe her jitters. The time before her next hit somehow seemed longer, because she had to share with Lou. The paranoia began to reach into the crevices of her brain. "I know I've been doing extra hits!" she protested aloud.

She sat topless in front of the computer, reluctant to remain in a bedroom with two naked men. She logged on to Pogo.com and chose a hidden object game to occupy her time and steady her shaking nerves. She grumbled again under her breath, "They better not smoke extra hits without me."

"Amy!" Ryan shouted from the bedroom. Hearing the pitch of his voice, she leaped from her computer and ran to the bedroom. "Yeah, I hear you. It's finally my turn," she mumbled. Returning to the bedroom, she found Ryan holding the pipe while Lou stood stroking his penis and sweating profusely. Neither of them had a hard-on. She gave them a disgusted look and said, "It's about time."

"What's wrong?" Ryan said. "You think we're doing hits without you?"

"It did cross my mind," she replied sternly. "Maybe I should stay in here, where I can watch both of you."

"Stay in here with us," Lou begged. As she sat on the bed and stared at the TV screen, not comprehending what she was seeing, she smoked another hit. Ryan and Lou passed the pipe again. Ryan walked to each window in the bedroom and took a lengthy peek outside. The crack abuse began to intensify his paranoia. Amy stepped up to the bureau and smoked another hit.

"Pull down your pants, Amy," Lou asked in an encouraging tone. "Get naked with us."

Amy glared at Ryan discouragingly. He smiled at her. "Go ahead get naked," he urged.

High and erotic from the crack rush, she pulled her blue shorts down over her ankles. She kicked them off and stood alongside of them, dressed only in black lace panties. "Okay, now the panties," Ryan said, pushing back a loose strand of blond hair from his forehead.

"No! I think this is enough for now." She took another hit and returned to her computer. The guys continued to get high until they finished all the packages. Lou made his usual drink and promptly left.

* * *

Ryan's keen business intellect afforded him certain advantages Amy lacked. He made his own work schedule, and, although she earned more than he did, he began to slack off with his business. He failed to get more clients, because he took more days off than he actually worked.

When Thursday rolled around, he did not have enough money to pay back Lou. Lou called early Thursday morning looking for his money, but Ryan let the answering machine do his talking. It took Ryan three weeks and four voice messages to reimburse Lou.

The next weekend, Ryan called Junior and Nokie. Neither of them returned his calls. Ryan believed luck was on his side to escape detection, because he always made the dealers come to the apartment. All of his transactions took place behind closed doors and windows. When his dealers ignored his calls, he had no recourse left. He called a different friend that he used to get high with every so often.

"Hey, Lenny. What's up?" he said into the receiver.

"Not much, Ryan. How are you doing?" was the response.

"I'm good. I thought if you'd hook me up I'd give you a couple of whacks."

"Yeah sure, pick me up in half an hour."

Ryan picked Lenny up forty-five minutes later, and they drove to Chelsea. Lenny scored a quarter-ounce, and on the way home he wanted to do a whack.

"Hey, asshole, do you think you can wait fifteen fucking minutes until we get back to Quincy?" Ryan screeched.

"Don't worry, it will be fine," Lenny reassured him.

After passing through the Tobin Bridge tolls, Lenny took a glass cigar tube out of his pocket. He had already filled the bottom of it with baking soda before entering the car. He poured one package in the tube and added some Poland Spring water he had found in the console of Ryan's car.

"What the fuck are you doing, asshole?" Ryan screamed. "Stop being a fucking idiot!"

Ryan, ignoring his own addiction, realized how bad other addictions were and the way they drive most people to stupidity. Lenny had no idea of the consequences, and if he had, he did not seem to care. Ryan drove down Route 93 toward Quincy on a dark moonless night as Lenny lit the tube and cooked the coke.

"What the fuck, Lenny! We're driving down a dark road in a dark car, and you're flicking the fucking lighter! We look like a fucking lighthouse, spitting out flashes of light every three seconds!"

"No worries man. Just drive while I do one hit," he told Ryan, jonesing for that first whack.

"Talk about drawing attention to ourselves!" Ryan retorted. "You act as if you're looking to get pinched by the cops! You're asking for trouble, asshole! Put that the fucking tube away before I kick you out of this car right here, right now!"

Ryan was so pissed he dropped Lenny off at his house and told him, "Instead of coming home with me, just take what you have in the tube." Ryan brought the rest home to Amy.

The Friday after the Lenny incident, Ryan and Amy needed to get high, but had no cash left. Ryan owed his mother and all of his friends. No more cash was available on the credit cards, and they had exhausted all of their options. Their favorite pizza palace was out, because they had bounced a check there the previous Friday.

* * *

Ryan's unmarried brother, Robert, lived with his girlfriend in Randolph, and the two of them drank vodka like swilling Russians from Siberia. Robert had joined the United States Marine Corps right after high school and completed two tours in Vietnam. Like most men in combat, he suffered from post-traumatic stress disorder and had returned home less of a man than when he had left. He looked exactly like Ryan, with eyes of a cold winter sky and blond hair shaped in a military crew cut. Across his left forearm was a *USMC First to Fight* tattoo, and on the other arm he had tattooed *Kill or be killed*.

He lived every day as though it was his last, and those who met him instantly fell under his magical charm, including Amy. Robert received monthly disability checks from the government, which covered all of his living expenses. He lacked gainful employment, and a typical day started with a glass of vodka, scratching lottery tickets at his favorite convenience store, and drinking with the boys at his local veterans lodge. Ryan had a solid relationship with his brother and knew Robert easily had enough to lend him something.

Ryan snapped the footrest of the recliner and stood up. "I'm going to take a ride and see Robert," he declared. Then he asked Amy, "Do you want me to bring you back anything?" as she settled down on the couch to watch television.

"Yes, if you get any money from Robert, I'd like you to get me a pack of Marlboros," she said with a crinkled nose. They owed so much money she had difficulty even thinking about borrowing more. She hated to borrow money and imagined it would take years to pay everyone back, but the devil's hold was too strong. She needed to get high, and every time she took a hit, the worries of the bills disappeared.

Ryan slipped on his jacket, grabbed his car keys, and drove to Randolph. He arrived at Robert's house twenty minutes later and rang the doorbell.

"Hey bro, what's up? Come on in," Robert said with a smile and a shot of vodka in his hand.

Ryan walked over the threshold and gave his brother a five-second masculine hug with two quick slaps on the back. "Hey guy, what's up?"

"Can I get you a drink?" Robert asked, closing the door.

"Of course brother. I'll take a beer."

"Have a seat," Robert said, motioning to his frayed, discolored couch. "I'll get you that beer." Robert turned toward the kitchen and yelled out to Ryan, "My girlfriend is out shopping, so we have about an hour to chat."

Robert had lived with her on and off for almost ten years, but the family disliked her because she encouraged her boyfriend's alcoholism. Halfway through the month, when he had depleted his government check on booze, she had disappeared for days and did not return until the appearance of his next month's check. The family knew she appeared in Robert's life only when there was money in his pocket.

After Ryan and Robert had spent an hour shooting the shit, Ryan turned to his brother. "I'm sorry to bother you, but I need to borrow some money." He shook his head in disgust, knowing he was about to deceive his brother. "I got a new job, and I start on Monday, but I don't have any cash. Can you lend me a few bucks?" He smirked, appealing to Robert's understanding and good will. "I'll pay you back when I get paid," he reassured him. It was the first day of the month, and Ryan hoped Robert hadn't drunk his check away. When Robert put his hand in his back pocket and pulled out his wallet, Ryan relaxed.

"How much do you need?" Robert unfolded his wallet and pulled out a wad of cash.

"I need a C-note," Ryan said, looking down at the stack of hundreds in his brother's hand.

"Done deal," Robert said, handing Ryan two hundred dollars. "Keep it. You don't need to pay me back."

"Don't worry. I'll get it back to you when I can."

Robert shook his head, "I mean it. I don't want it back. You don't owe me a thing. Just sit down and have a drink with me." He turned toward the kitchen to mix drinks. Feeling obligated, Ryan followed him, pulled a chair from the kitchen table, and took a seat.

The brothers drank two beers together and shot the shit for an hour. Then Ryan shoved his empty glass across the table. "I have to get going. Amy is home, waiting for me." The guilt weighed on Ryan, because he knew the power of the devil was coming before his love for his brother. He pushed his chair from the table and said, "Semper-Fi, bro. Gotta go."

"Semper, it was good to see you. Don't be a stranger, and give my love to Amy. We should have dinner soon," Robert said, rising from the table and giving his brother a hard handshake.

Ryan walked to the door and, with a second thought, lifted his head back toward Robert and hollered, "Tell your girl I said hi!" As he walked out the door, he heard Robert yell out, "Okay!"

Ryan drove up Route 28 from Randolph to Quincy in fifteen minutes and called Nokie from his cell phone. He arrived home just in time to see Nokie pull in the driveway.

"What's up, man? How many you need?" Nokie asked, giving him a slap of the hand.

"Not out here. Come in the house," Ryan said, leading him in. As soon as they entered, Ryan sat at the kitchen table. "I need three, and look, the last time the shit wasn't very good. Let me see what you have this time."

Nokie handed him six packages.

"No, man, I want to see everything." Nokie took the large Ziploc bag and dumped it on the kitchen table. Twenty packages spewed out; three landed on the Oriental rug. "Now that's much better," Ryan said, aware of the three on the floor. Nokie never saw them. Ryan picked three decent-sized packages from the table. "Thanks, man," he said as he forked over a C-note. "See you next time."

"Okay, later man," he smiled. Nokie slid the remaining packages in a large Baggie and left without counting them.

Ryan laughed excitedly. "I don't fucking believe it, Amy. We finally got a break."

She stared at him in confusion. "What are you talking about?"

He bent over, picked up the three on the floor, and showed them to Amy. She looked stunned. "Where did those come from? How did you afford all of this? What, you have extra money I don't know about?" She did not mind having the extra packages, but would be upset if Ryan spent more money than they had to lose.

"When Nokie dumped the baggie on the table, three fell to the floor," he explained.

"No way! You're kidding."

"Do I look like I'm kidding? You know how much cash I got from Robert? And I didn't have any when I left."

"Cool. Cook them up, and we'll get started."

Ten minutes after their first hit, the telephone rang. "Shit, that has to be him," he told Amy.

"What are we going to do?"

"Nothing," he said. "Just let the answering machine pick it up."

It did, five seconds later. "Hey man, it's Nokie. You were a bad boy. I know you took three, because

I counted them, and I know what I had. Pick up, man." The message went silent for a few seconds. "Come on, man, I need that money. Shit! Okay, but I'm not doing business with you again until you pay me what you owe me."

Ryan and Amy heard the "hang up" click and started to laugh. "It's going to be one hell of a night," he said as he lifted the pipe to his mouth. "We better enjoy it while it lasts."

Heather McCarthy

CALIFORNIA DISASTER

Amy understood how crack cocaine conveys an image of a hip, upscale drug used by individuals from all walks of life, including high achievers, but this did not matter to her. It attracts the high-powered professional, and Ryan and Amy exemplified this behavior by establishing a definite routine. They seemed to be high most weekends and at least two days during the week, but managed to function normally on a daily basis, continuing to arrive at work on time and occasionally enjoying a customary lifestyle with a date night once a month.

By the time the 1998 Winter Olympic Games rolled around, their bills were three months overdue. They emptied their savings account and continued to borrow money from family and friends, as if they were a bank. Their life was spiraling in a downward pirouette.

In May, Amy retrieved her Internal Revenue check from the mailbox. Hence, if the depletion of her wedding purse and savings account happened to be any indication, she did not intend to blow that two thousand dollars. She placed it in a six-month Certificate of Deposit, earning six and one-half percent interest and ensuring its safety from withdrawal during a crack binge.

Fifteen years earlier, Ryan's good friend from high school, Gary Roberts, had relocated to California. Gary managed a posh Ford Dealership in Redondo Beach. In September, he returned home to Quincy for a short visit with his parents. He scheduled visits with his friends, who included Ryan.

The telephone chimed four times before Amy had a chance to reach the receiver. She ran through the living room, tripped over the coffee table, and lifted the handset.

"Hello?" she said.

"Hello, is Ryan at home?" the caller inquired with a deep, sexy voice. An image of Richard Gere's portrayal of Julian Kane in *American Gigolo* flooded her mind.

"Just a moment. I'll get him." She laid the handset down on the table and called out, "Hey, Ryan! It's for you!"

Ryan appeared from the bedroom, where he had been watching the New England Patriots kick ass against the Arizona Cardinals, thirty-one to nothing. He walked to the phone.

"Hello. Who's this?" he inquired, agitated that someone had interrupted him during such an exciting game.

"Hey, buddy, its Gary. It's been a long time."

"Hey, brother, what's up? Yeah, been a long time. Are you calling from Cal?" He had pleasure and excitement in his voice.

"No, man, I'm here in Quincy. I have another five days, and wanted to see if we could hook up while I'm in town."

"Of course we can, you asshole," Ryan laughed. "I would hope you wouldn't leave town without stopping by to see me. What day do you want to get together? I'm not busy this week, so any day is good for me."

"What about tomorrow night? I have no plans, and I thought we could watch the L.A. Raiders."

"Perfect. Come by for dinner, and you can meet my wife, the lovely Amy. Take Granite Street to Whitwell, and right on Glendale. It's number twenty-three. See you soon, bro."

He replaced the handset to its base and turned to Amy. "That was my good friend Gary. He moved to California years ago, and he's back in town for a few days, so I invited him for dinner. You don't mind, do you? He's a good friend, and you'll love him."

"No, not at all, but I have to get some sleep after working all night. I suppose I should call in sick."

"Screw it, call in sick. We'll have a good time. I'll get a couple of packages, and Gary can tell us all about Cal."

She eyed her husband curiously. "He smokes crack too?"

"No, No, No! He snorts lines. Don't ever mention it to him that we smoke the shit. Don't ever tell anyone we do. Do you hear me?"

"Yeah, I hear you, but why not?"

"Because, for one, I don't think he's cool, and second, because I don't want anyone to know my business," he snapped firmly.

Amy's body fell loose. "Okay." For the first time

since starting to smoke crack, she realized Ryan always seemed to find a reason to get high. The next morning, she called in sick.

Gary jumped out of the shower, blew-dry his hair, and put on a blue Ralph Lauren Polo shirt with designer jeans. He dressed meticulously and always agonized over his appearance. He wore only the best, but his muscular physique and dark features turned heads no matter what he wore. He grabbed his wallet and keys from the bureau, and ran out the door headed for Ryan's apartment.

Gary adjusted to life in Los Angeles shortly after he moved, but his return to Quincy made him homesick for the uncomplicated side of life. His parents hoped he would stay home permanently, but they raised him as an independent, freethinking individual. He loved Los Angeles, and it is where he made his living.

He arrived at the apartment at five o'clock and knocked on the door three times. He stared impatiently at the door before knocking again, when Ryan appeared. In a manly stance, Gary and Ryan hugged each other for several minutes while patting one another on the back.

"Hey man, come in and meet the wife," Ryan exclaimed. "It's good to see you. You look great. California does you justice."

As he stepped over the threshold, Amy's eyes dropped to the floor as a Richard Gere lookalike stood before her. The voice she heard on the telephone equaled his dark hair, coffee eyes, and gorgeous muscular body. "Hello there," she whispered so no one heard. Ryan made all the introductions, and with the proper tone she appropriately said, "Hello."

With ease Amy prepared the table for dinner and served her specialty of eggplant Parmesan with tender bowtie pasta. They spent an hour eating, drinking, and laughing over good times. Because Gary managed a Ford dealership, he knew all types of exciting people. They were mostly football players and movie stars.

Amy rose to clear the table of dirty dishes and sauce-stained placemats. "That was delicious," Ryan told her, and turned to Gary. "Now I have a little something for dessert. Let's head to the living room."

Ryan turned the television on to watch Monday night football and opened the decorative Hummel box where he hid the small bag of coke. He drew six lines on a small mirror he left on the coffee table. "Amy, we are ready!" he hollered into the kitchen.

She placed the dishes in the cabinet. The only disappointment in renting, instead of buying, was the small cabinets and lack of storage space, but she managed to find a spot for everything. She walked by the kitchen table, blew out the tall red candles, and sat on the couch beside Ryan.

They took turns snorting lines, drinking cocktails, and watching the L.A. Raiders. "You guys need to come out to L.A. soon," Gary urged them during halftime. "I'll take care of everything. I have a big house, and you can stay with me. You can visit Disneyland, the San Diego Zoo, and Knott's Berry

Farm. I'll take you down Rodeo Drive and over to Universal Studios. We'll have a good time."

"Sounds like a *great* time," Ryan replied. "I've never been to Cal, and I'd love to go." He looked down at the plate of coke as he drew three more lines. He turned to Amy. "What do you think? Wanna go?"

"I'd love to go," she said. "I flew out there once, back in the eighties, but I'm not sure we have the money."

"Let's go next February at tax time, and use our tax refund," Ryan suggested. "It'll be awesome to get away from the cold for a week, and Gary will put us up. Let's go."

"I mean it, Amy," Gary urged. "I'll take care of everything. You won't have to spend a dime. You just need to spring for airfare."

"Okay, sounds good to me," she spouted with an absorbing look. What she really looked forward to was a trip to California and a healthy vacation.

The three snorted more lines and drank until midnight, when Gary left. He flew back to Cal Friday afternoon and made a final telephone call to remind them to come out for a visit. Amy went to bed late that night, excited about taking a vacation, for they had not left the city since their honeymoon.

When January rolled around, she cashed out the money in the certificate of deposit. The time had come to use it. After filing their taxes, she anticipated another thousand coming back to them, which would be more than enough for a vacation in California. She booked a flight on Delta Airlines a week later, using her credit card. She knew that by the time the bill arrived she would have her refund check.

Smiling in delight, Amy danced provocatively through the living room to "Like a Virgin" by Madonna. She knew it would be a whole week away from the crack. She whispered into the air, "Time away will provide us with an opportunity to wean off the crack." For months their routine remained the same, and by the time she was ready to pack, she couldn't wait to get out of town.

On an early frigid morning the following February, Ryan and Amy flew Delta out of Boston's Logan airport with a stopover in Detroit and on to LAX. At two in the afternoon, California time, they landed at LAX airport with a hard thump. Ryan spent the flight with a couple of cocktails while Amy spent her time snoozing. They wanted to get off the plane in a hurry to start their vacation. He rose from his seat, and she followed as soon as the captain turned off the seatbelt sign, but the fifteen passengers in front of them moved as if they wore cement shoes specifically designed by the Mafia. The other passengers stuffed the overhead bins, and they waited impatiently for the passengers in front of them. It was hot, the other passengers around them smelled of sweat, and Amy needed a cigarette.

She got on the conveyor belt in front of her husband. "That was the longest flight I've ever taken," he said. "I'm still having trouble trying to straighten out my knees."

"Yes, I thought so too," she chuckled, "but you

enjoyed the flight, right?"

Yeah, I love to fly, especially when it's with you. I love you."

"And I love you too. Do you think Gary will be there waiting?"

"I hope so. I hate waiting around in airports, and I hope the turnstile doesn't take forever to dump our suitcases," he said, gaining on her as he started to walk faster on the electric walkway.

After twenty minutes, they arrived at the baggage turnstile, and as they waited for it to turn they searched for Gary. Ryan noticed a tall man in a chauffeur's uniform holding a large sign that read "O'CONNOR" in big letters.

"You've got to be shitting me," Ryan exclaimed. "I told you Gary would take care of us, but I didn't expect this. This is going to be a wonderful vacation." He bent down and kissed her softly on the lips. "I love you. You know that, don't you?" he asked.

Amy nodded a genuine surprise and agreed with Ryan. "And I love you too," she said as a smile and a pink flush warmed her face.

Ryan approached the chauffeur. "Hello," he said. "We are the O'Connor's."

"Good afternoon," the chauffeur said. "Where are you coming from?" He was of Mexican ancestry, meticulously dressed, and Amy caught a whiff of his expensive after-shave, though she did not place the scent with a name.

"We live in Quincy," Ryan answered. "It's just south of Boston."

"Very good," he remarked as he reached for the suitcases. He lifted them onto a Smart Cart with a little help from Ryan and led them outside to a black stretch limousine. He opened the door. "My name is José, welcome to Los Angeles," he said. "It will be around twenty-five minutes to Mr. Roberts' home in San Pedro. He left everything you'll need for the journey in the back seat. He's running late and suggested you open the small storage compartment on the back right door for your entertainment pleasure."

"Thank you very much," Ryan said with a handshake as he motioned for Amy to slide into the back seat. As the chauffeur closed the door and placed the luggage in the trunk, Ryan slid into the limo and lifted the storage compartment. "Man, I don't believe him," he whispered in surprise.

"Why, what's in there?" Amy asked inquisitively.

Ryan pulled out a plastic baggie containing an eight ball. Amy's smile faded to a bittersweet frown. She anticipated a coke-free week in the hope Ryan would slow down, but now the hopes shattered in disappointment. Ryan opened the package, and they snorted a couple of lines. He served two drinks from the portable bar.

The limousine pulled out of LAX and veered south down Pacific Coast Highway toward Manhattan Beach. Ryan and Amy glanced out the tinted windows at the lush scenery and towns tucked along the shoreline. José drove along the seaside homes of Manhattan Beach, Hermosa and Redondo

Beach, and traveled down Ocean Boulevard pass the Portofino Inn. The sunlit hillsides in the distance were picturesque of the Hollywood Riviera. The limo driver ascended to Palos Verdes and Rolling Hills. He rounded the peninsula pass the Hanna-Barbera Marineland and down into San Pedro, making a stop at the Korean Bell for pictures.

"Korea presented the bell to American to celebrate Americas bicentennial," José explained. "It is a symbol of friendship, and the city dedicated it in October of seventy-six."

As Ryan and Amy gazed from the hills of San Pedro at the clear ocean stretching to Catalina Island, they snorted a few more lines. "Take your shirt off and play with your nipples," he told her.

"No! The driver will see," she said. Ryan pressed the power button and raised the tinted partition between the driver and them. Amy lifted her blouse, pushed her hands inside her bra, and lifted each breast one at a time to her mouth. She sucked on each one to make them wet and tickled her nipples with her thumbs.

As Ryan watched Amy squeeze her nipples, his penis began to pulsate. He leaned into her face, gave her a peck on the cheek, and cupped her breasts in his hands. He yanked them out from under her bra. He took her nipples in his mouth and sucked hard. She squirmed, and her panties became wet with her juices. He slid his hand up her skirt and into her panties. He explored her clit and manipulated her until she came.

"What about a beana?" he asked. It was his slang

term for a blowjob. "I never got one in a limo before."

"No, now stop it," she snapped. "I think we are getting close to Gary's house." She pushed his hand away, straightened her skirt, and lowered her blouse.

"You've never been here before. What makes you think we're close?" he said in a humiliating tone, as if she was ignorant.

"I'm sorry if I upset you, but we have been driving for more than twenty-five minutes, so I just assumed we were close," she reasoned. "You do not need to take a condescending tone with me."

"Well, I think you should stop assuming things and wait until we get there."

Amy ignored him, turned her face away, and looked out the tinted window. A tiny tear filled her eyes. In the distance, as they approached Gary's home, a magnificent view of the Port of Los Angeles with a dominating skyline of soaring cranes and storage containers astounded them. Amy remembered Gary saying, "The famous port is the site of three commercial fishing piers." They looked at marinas jam-packed with luxury yachts as well as two cruise ships. On this particular warm Sunday, parades of sailboats and fishing trawlers made their way inside the harbor, causing Ryan and Amy to dream of a better life. Amy suddenly remembered her father telling her to never stop dreaming.

After Ryan and Amy snorted a few more lines and sipped on another glass of champagne, Ryan reopened the partition and asked José, "Hey, man, can you stop at a local market? I would like to buy a few items for the house."

José stopped at Vons Market and opened their doors as if they were royalty. Ryan walked into a crowded market and quickly picked up a bottle of vodka, rum, mixers, potato chips, and ice cream. He jumped back into the limo and snorted another line as José continued down a couple of rights and a final left.

On a serene street with no traffic sat Gary's home—a beautiful large sapphire two-story dwelling with white trim, a meticulously maintained lawn, flowerpots, and rosebushes arranged along the walkway. José stopped, parked alongside the lawn, and opened his door.

Amy reached for the door handle when Ryan grabbed her hand. "No, Amy," he demanded. "Let the driver get it. It's his job."

The driver opened Amy's door. She strolled up the cobbled walkway, ascended the three steps to the main entrance, located the key under the welcome mat and unlocked the door. Removing her sunglasses, she ventured in the living room.

After tipping José two twenties, Ryan followed close behind her with suitcases in hand. "Where should we leave the suitcases?" she asked Ryan while peering in at a well-furnished living room.

"Just leave them on the floor by the couch, out of the way, until Gary gets home," he instructed her. "He will tell us where they belong." He did not want to disrupt Gary's home without his approval.

Amy put down the bags and looked around with a sigh of relief. Her eyes sparkled with delight in knowing they had finally arrived. She looked forward to having a fun time. Amy knew they had been in a rut since starting to smoke crack, never leaving the apartment, and staring at four walls every day became gloomy, isolated, and boring.

Amy stood at the foot of the couch and glanced out the large bay window. She saw a spectacular view of the ocean and the Port of Los Angeles. "Ryan," she called out to him. "Check this out. It is amazing."

Ryan approached the window. "Wow, It's awesome." He stood looking at the view for more than a moment. He turned to her, hugged her, and kissed her on the forehead. "We're going to have a great time. I'm so glad Gary invited us." He walked away softly singing "I Left My Heart in San Francisco" by Tony Bennett.

Amy turned from the window and walked through the living room, checking out Gary's décor. Against the wall she found a stunning red brick fireplace. With a puzzled look she turned to Ryan and asked him, "Why would anyone need a fireplace in California?"

Ryan shrugged his shoulders. "Beats me."

She shook her head slightly and walked into the adjoining dining room, glancing at its high-end indigo carpeting, then back at the dark cherry wood dining set in the middle of the living room.

The modern kitchen with black marble flooring and matching countertops stood against the right wall of the dining room, with a laundry room to the left. She found Gary's home immaculate and unusual for a bachelor. She placed the grocery bags on the countertop beside the refrigerator, unpacked them, placed the dry goods in the beige-colored cupboards, and put the booze in the refrigerator along with the mixers.

Ryan followed closely behind her. "Hey, don't put the booze in the refrigerator, I want a drink!" he scolded her as if she was a child. Again, she just ignored him, knowing it was the coke talking, not him. He stopped the refrigerator door with his forearm to keep it from closing and removed the booze. "What's the matter with you? I'm on vacation, and I want to start drinking heavily," he said with a hearty laugh. "Don't you want a drink?" he asked, glaring at her curiously. He did not understand her motives for putting the booze away without making a drink. For an intelligent woman with a college degree, he thought she acted quite stupid at times.

"Okay, you're right. Make me one, too," she said, opening the freezer and shoving the ice cream next to the ice cubes. Ryan opened the cabinets and removed two tall crystal glasses, placed them on the countertop, and poured a shot of vodka with a large splash of cranberry juice.

As she sipped her drink she walked down a narrow hallway beyond the kitchen. She took pleasure in the taste. "This is good. Ryan makes a smooth cocktail," she said quietly under her breath. To the left she found a staircase leading to the upper floors but avoided venturing up the stairs. Past the staircase she found a full-size guest bedroom, a small, adorable bedroom, and an office with a desk and a computer. Adjacent to the office she entered a delightful sunroom with wicker-style furniture and French doors. She opened them and stepped on the deck, which had a gas grill. She sniffed an overpowering aroma of roses and turned to her left, where she noticed several pink rosebushes along a white picket fence.

To the right of the rosebushes, Amy noticed a four-car garage. She bent down and smelled the beautiful petals, then walked to the garage door, opened it, and peered into a cozy refinished room. The garage held several wall shelves with plenty of storage space and a wide collection of NFL sports memorabilia spanning three decades, which Gary had acquired while working for a photographer who serviced an AFC contender.

Returning to the French doors, she reentered the sunroom and walked back to the kitchen with an empty glass. "What a lovely home Gary has. I love it," Amy remarked to Ryan, opening her emerald irises in awe.

Ryan saw her empty glass. "I'm empty, too. Want another drink?" he offered.

"Yes, I think I do. Thank you."

They took their drinks and promptly made a toast to California. "Here's to a long awaited vacation," Ryan proposed, lifting his glass high in the air.

"Yes, here's to California," she agreed, raising her crystal and tapping it against Ryan's.

"Gary does all right for himself," Ryan informed her with an immense smile. "He works at a huge dealership with rich clientele."

Amy picked up the suitcases from the living room floor and, after choosing the full-sized bedroom, unpacked them while Ryan made them another vodka and cranberry. They sat at the dining-room table, which was loaded with mail, two days' worth of the *San Pedro Daily*, and a small pile of papers Amy disregarded. It was none of her business.

Ryan grabbed a dark-covered magazine from the coffee table and drew out four lines onto it. Half of the eight ball seemed to disappear during the drive, and Ryan said in a stunned tone, "We will just do these six and save the rest for Gary. I'm sure he'll want a line when he gets home."

Amy nodded in agreement. As soon as they started to snort the lines, the telephone rang twice, and the answering machine spewed out a message. After the annoying tone had wailed, they heard, "Hey, guys, just wanted to make sure…" The message broke off as Ryan picked up the handset.

"Hey, brother," Ryan said. "Yeah, we're in, and everything's cool. Okay, sure thing." He hung up. Turning to Amy, he said, "He called to make sure we arrived safely and got settled. He said to take the guest bedroom downstairs, and he'll be home in twenty-five minutes. He wants to get Chinese." Ryan turned on the stereo, sat at the table with Amy, finished his cocktail and quickly poured another.

Gary arrived on time. "Hey guys," he said as he strode through the sunroom French doors, hugged Ryan and kissed Amy. "So glad you're here. How was the flight? Did you find the limo okay?"

"Everything was wonderful, and gotta love the little surprise in the back seat," Ryan said.

"The flight seemed to last forever, and I'm a bit tired, but the house is beautiful, and the view from the bay window is absolutely gorgeous," Amy remarked with sincerity.

"Hey Gary, you ready for a line?" Ryan continued.

"No, not yet. Let me get situated first and clean up a little bit. I'll be with you in a few."

Gary trotted up the staircase, taking two stairs at a time with the ease of a gazelle. Amy lifted her head to the ceiling as energetic footsteps danced above her head. The water from the shower hummed in her ears.

Forty-five minutes later, Gary descended the stair, wearing exquisite cologne. She cocked her head and sniffed the air around him as the aroma astounded her.

Amy stored the toiletries in the bathroom while Gary and Ryan sat at the dining-room table, enjoying a cocktail. "Gary, this home is beautiful!" Amy yelled from the bathroom. "I'm so jealous! You have decorated it wonderfully!"

"Thank you, and please consider it your home away from home," Gary insisted. "Ryan already has a line waiting for you. I'm going to wait until after dinner."

"Well, I don't want one if we're having dinner!" she hollered again.

"Who wants to eat after snorting coke?" Ryan

remarked annoyingly. He did not understand Amy. After years of marriage and smoking crack, why did she not recognize that he hated to eat before getting high?

"I do," Gary said firmly with a smile. "I just got out of work, and I'm hungry. I thought pizza instead of Chinese would be a better idea. I'll order and have it delivered. What kind do you like?" He reached for the telephone next to the table and dialed.

"I'd like pepperoni," Amy responded as she appeared from the bathroom. "What about you?" she asked her husband. "What do you want?"

"I won't eat much, so order whatever you like," he snapped in irritation.

Gary turned the television on to watch football. During the commercials, Ryan and Amy listened to him talk about his divorce and all the plans he made for their vacation. The pizza arrived twenty minutes later. The three sat at the dining room table, talked over old times and, after they finished eating, snorted the rest of the eight ball. Amy bonded with Gary instantly. Ryan poured them glasses of rum and Coke before bed.

Ascending the staircase, Gary stopped and turned to his guests. "Hey, guys, I'm not working tomorrow, and I want to take you for lunch and some sightseeing. So see you in the morning."

The next morning, Amy awoke to the intoxicating aroma of brewing coffee and the sun streaming through the bedroom windows. She did not want Gary to see her in a tousled first-morning appearance, so she showered, dressed, and applied her makeup. She understood the reason for the fireplace; the house was chilly.

She strolled to the kitchen, where Gary was drinking coffee and reading the newspaper at the breakfast nook. "Good morning," she said.

"Good morning. I hope you slept well," he replied, his eyes glued to his paper.

"Oh, yes, wonderfully. That bed has to be the most comfortable one I have ever slept in," she told him as she poured herself a cup of coffee. "It seems a bit chilly this morning."

"I can start the fireplace if you like, but the sun warms up the house fairly quickly," he told her, his head still in the periodical. "The house will be warm by ten o'clock."

"Oh no, it's fine." She did not want him to go through the trouble of starting a fire.

He turned to her and smiled. "I have to go out and do a few errands, so after you guys have breakfast, I'll take you sightseeing, and I know a good place where we can have lunch. It's right on the ocean."

* * *

Gary drove Ryan and Amy around San Pedro on a magic carpet ride back around the peninsula. He showed them the beach cities of Redondo, Hermosa, and Manhattan and ended the tour in Marina Del Ray. He entered the freeway toward Beverly Hills and Rodeo Drive. He took a forty-minute spin on a sun-kissed day of adventure, revealing to his guests how stylish California is, with an anything-goes attitude.

The three strolled slowly down Rodeo Drive, taking in its glittering shops and Oscar-winning fashions. "I wonder if we'll see any movie stars," Amy pondered.

"You might, but they hardly ever come here because of the tourists," Gary told her. "All of the celebrities usually send their personal maids and butlers."

Amy walked into a couple of the boutiques but came out empty-handed. "Why didn't you buy something?" Ryan asked her as they continued to walk. "Didn't you see anything you liked?"

"I liked everything, but the stores are very expensive. There wasn't one thing I can afford. A souvenir coffee cup was twenty dollars."

"Don't worry about it, just charge it. We are on vacation, damn it. Have fun."

When they returned to the car, Gary drove down Sunset Boulevard through Pacific Palisades to Gladstone's on Malibu Beach for a quick bite, where they saw Jack Klugman from the seventies sitcom *The Odd Couple.* Overall, the day turned out glorious for all of them.

While sitting at a booth in Gladstone's, Gary turned to Ryan and asked him, "Would you like me to call the mailman when we get home?"

"Sure, sounds like a plan," Ryan responded.

Amy stared at them with a confusing glare. "What do you mean by the mailman?" she asked.

"It's Gary's phrase for getting a package," Ryan

snickered. "Gary puts the money in the mailbox, calls his guy, and his connection replaces the money in the mailbox with a package, alias the mailman." She found it quite *apropos* and chuckled.

After arriving home, Gary called his dealer and placed the money in the mailbox. He pulled a large-sized Baggie out from a hidden drawer under the coffee table.

"You guys ready for a joint?" he asked his guests.

"Sure," Ryan said excitedly.

Gary and Ryan sat lounging around the living room, smoking a joint, watching a football game and drinking Coors beer. Gary passed the joint to Amy.

"She doesn't smoke pot," Ryan said.

"Yeah, not since college," she said. "It makes me paranoid, and I eat myself out of house and home. I gain five pounds for every joint." She giggled.

"I don't think you need to worry about your weight. You look just fine to me," Gary told her.

"Thanks, you're such a charmer."

The three waited patiently for the mailman to deliver the package. "I commandeered a vehicle this morning so you can drive to San Diego and check out the zoo," he informed them.

"Sounds great, it should be a lot of fun," Amy responded energetically with an ear-to-ear smile.

Twenty minutes went by when Gary lifted his head to the sound of the mailbox lid opening and closing. "The mail's been delivered." They all chuckled.

"Gary, do you mind if I take half the package and

cook it?" Ryan asked.

"No, I guess not. You smoke it?" Gary inquired with a concerned frown.

"Yeah, once in a while," Ryan told him coyly.

"Yeah sure, go ahead," Gary said indifferently. "It's none of my business. Do what you like." He wanted them to enjoy their vacation. He was cool with whatever they planned. Meanwhile, Amy stared at Ryan, remembering him telling her not to tell. She shook her head in disbelief, acknowledging the double standard between men and women.

Ryan cooked half the eight ball as Gary and Amy munched on a cheeseburger and potato chips with pickles. After dinner, the gag reflexes took over, affecting all three of them, causing an outburst of laughter. Gary made a rum and Coke for Amy and grabbed two more beers, one for himself and another for Ryan. "Okay, let's take our drinks and go do a hit," Ryan said.

They disappeared into the bedroom with the plate of crack. Ryan stripped and passed the pipe to Amy. She took her hit, returned the pipe to Ryan, and joined Gary in the living room. He snorted his lines and played solitaire.

"Do you want to play Spades?" she asked. "I get too antsy just sitting around doing nothing."

Gary's eyes widened with delight. "It sounds good to me."

All through the game, she twisted nervously back and forth in her seat. She turned her head toward the bedroom every few seconds, itching to leave the game and get another hit. Suddenly, she heard gagging from Ryan. It sounded harder than usual. She tilted her neck up and perked her ears toward the bedroom. She heard him dart to the bathroom and vomit in the toilet. She looked at Gary. "Something is wrong. He never throws up when he's getting high."

"Maybe you should check to see if he's all right," he said quickly.

She stood up. "I'll be right back." She crossed into the kitchen and opened the bathroom door—no Ryan. She turned and entered the bedroom, finding him there.

"What is the matter with you? Are you okay?" she asked, approaching him with genuine concern.

"I don't feel good. I just threw up. I'm not sure what's wrong," he mumbled, turning away from her as he ran to the john again. She raised her ears closer to the forcible sound of gagging.

Returning to the dining room, she whimpered in despair, "Gary, he's throwing his guts up. I've never seen him this sick. I'm not sure what to do,"

Gary glanced blankly at her as if in deep thought. "I'm sure I have something in the medicine cabinet for him." He ran upstairs to the master bedroom, coming down a few seconds later with a package of Tums and a bottle of Pepto-Bismol. "Here try this," he said, opening the Tums and handing her the Pepto.

Amy returned to the bedroom and caught Ryan doing another hit. "Are you okay now?" she asked him. "I brought you something for your stomach." She handed him the medicines.

"Yeah, I think so." He started to gag again and ran to the bathroom, throwing up once more. Amy placed the Pepto and the Tums on the dresser bureau, left the room and returned to Gary.

"He's throwing his guts up, but yet he's still smoking hits," she explained to Gary. "I don't know what to do with him."

"Just leave him alone," Gary persuaded her. "He's a big boy. He knows what he's doing. Snort a line and let's play another game."

She sat at the table, sniffed coke with Gary and dealt another hand. Meanwhile, Ryan took another hit and threw up again. She took a sip from her drink and ignored the vomiting noises until they finished the coke, at which point she rose from the table. "Goodnight, Gary," she said as she headed for the bedroom.

"Good night, and don't worry about him," he told her. "I'm sure he'll feel fine in the morning. It's been a long few days, and he must be tired or jet-lagged. Thanks for keeping me company."

"Sure, no problem, and thanks for everything. I had fun."

Ryan finished his last hit. The vomiting subsided, but his face looked chalky and drained. He tossed and turned all night, making it hard for Amy to sleep.

The next day they made plans to visit the San Diego Zoo, but Amy frowned with concern that Ryan might not make the trip, though he had told her more than once that he could.

The zoo opened at nine o'clock, and it was a

two-hour drive there via the freeway with a short stop in La Jolla, so Ryan and Amy left at eight. His stomach turned and growled for most of the drive, but he refused to turn back—after all, it was Amy's vacation. They drove directly to the zoo without stopping in La Jolla.

They had walked through two exhibits when Ryan turned to Amy and said, "I have to stop and get something to eat. After that, I want to go back to Gary's house."

"Okay, no problem. I knew you were too sick to come."

"Are you sure you don't mind? I'm sorry. I feel bad I'm screwing up your vacation."

"No, Ryan," she said unwaveringly. "It's not a problem. If you're sick, you're sick. I understand. I told you we shouldn't have come."

They stopped at Albert's restaurant for a bacon chicken grill and curly fries. Ryan ordered a glass of Merlot, and Amy ordered a Mojito. "Wow, I've never tasted one of these," she said. "They're pretty good."

"Do you think you can hurry it up? I feel like throwing up, and I wanna get out of here."

He never made it past the fries before he started to gag. He darted to the nearest bathroom. After half an hour, they left the restaurant for home. It had taken fifteen minutes and three vomiting attacks for him to reach the car.

As he cruised down the freeway, he maneuvered to the soft shoulder and stopped the car. He tried to vomit but managed only the dry heaves. Amy waited in the passenger seat and glanced out the window at the scenery. Thirty Marines in fatigues jogged past in the distance along the shoreline. Hearing the pulse of chop-chop-chop, she lifted her head to the sky. Two low-flying helicopters were hovering behind the jogging marines.

Ryan returned to the car. "Look at the helicopters," she told him, pointing upward. "They're so cool."

"We must be near Camp Pendleton," he remarked.

A few miles down the freeway, they passed the entrance to Camp Pendleton. Ryan turned to Amy. "See, I was right. Those must have been Marines on maneuvers. Now you can tell everyone at home you saw Camp Pendleton."

When they finally reached Gary's, a pink glow returned to Ryan's face, and his stomach quieted. He went to the freezer and spooned out a bowl of Breyers ice cream. It was a bad idea. He started to vomit all over again. By the time Gary arrived, Ryan was throwing up bile. "I think I need to go to the hospital," he told them. His face was ghostly pale, though it had a bronze shade from a slight tan.

"Hey, look, I have a friend who's a doctor, and I'll call him to see if we can get an appointment," Gary said as he picked up the telephone and dialed. After a short conversation, he hung up and turned to Ryan. "He can see you in twenty-five minutes," he said with a life-size smile and a soothing sound in his voice. "Get ready, and we will leave right away. He's ten minutes from here."

The doctor diagnosed Ryan with acute gastritis. He pumped a liter of fluid into him and gave him a "Happy Shot." Nobody had a clue about its components. The shot improved his nausea and his overall symptoms.

"This is a common ailment caused by excessive alcohol, dairy products, chocolate, and drug abuse," the doctor explained to Ryan. "You must not ingest any of these if you want to feel better. You may have small sips of water to keep you hydrated, but nothing else."

Around eight in the evening, Ryan got sick again and vomited three more times. He called to Amy from the bedroom, "Get me some ice cream! It will make me feel better!"

"Ryan, are you crazy? The doctor said no dairy products."

"I don't care! Get me some ice cream!" he demanded in a condescending tone.

"My husband is an asshole," Amy told Gary. "He's out of his mind, and there is no reasoning with him."

"Hey, buddy, the doctor said no ice cream!" Gary yelled toward the bedroom, "The doctor said just water and ginger ale, man! Come on, don't be stupid!"

Ignoring both of them, Ryan rushed to the freezer. He took a spoon from the kitchen drawer and scooped out a bowl of Sorbet's sherbet. He vomited five minutes later. After an hour of feeling like shit, he reached for the Tums and finally fell asleep.

The next four days passed miserably. Gary returned to work. Ryan spent the rest of his vacation in bed. Amy saw nothing of California, spending her afternoons watching television, playing solitaire, sitting on the deck taking in the smell of roses, and rummaging through the sports memorabilia in the garage.

California had turned disastrous. Amy wanted to go home. Whenever Ryan put anything in his stomach, he vomited. He had become violently ill one more time before Amy packed the suitcase. The doctor gave him another "Happy Shot" for the flight home. Ryan and Amy boarded a plane for Boston two days later and offered Gary a fond farewell.

HOME AGAIN

Ryan made the seven-hour flight home without incident, but as soon as they landed, he got sick again. The South Shore taxi dropped them off at the apartment. Ryan jumped out. "Give me the keys! I need to throw again!" he demanded. He opened the door and ran to the bathroom. Amy followed with the suitcases.

Emerging from the bathroom, Ryan ordered Amy, "You have to take me to the hospital right now!" He got into the passenger side of the car, and Amy drove him to Quincy Hospital as he sat gagging in the passenger seat. The emergency room doctor admitted him overnight and pumped him with substantial amounts of fluid. The lab report showed toxic levels of cocaine and marijuana in his bloodstream.

Ryan returned home the next afternoon, feeling well but tired. He remained at home the next week. After three days of recuperating, they spent the rest of their vacation money getting high—back to his jovial self, he forgot his illness and wanted a whack.

On one particular night a few weeks later, and after depleting their vacation money, they still wanted to get high. Amy left early for work, leaving her employer identification badge on the kitchen table. When she returned, she walked in and found Ryan smoking crack with Lou.

"What the fuck is going on here!" she shouted.

Ryan glared blankly at her, still feeling the rush from the hit he had just taken.

"What?" he answered, dumbfounded, with a blank stare and wide, round eyes. Lou stood beside him, drooling down the left side of his mouth.

"I thought we had no money left!" she shouted.

Ryan continued to glare at her, as though looking right through her. Lou returned to the bedroom for another hit, trying not to get involved.

"You're fucking high!" she snapped. "Come on, Ryan, what the fuck! Is *that* the reason we never have any money? This sucks. It's bad enough there's no money, but now you're getting high without me!" She turned, left the apartment, and slammed the door behind her.

Amy did not speak to Ryan for two days and refused to cough up any of her own money for the product. Her resentment toward Ryan deepened, and the wheels of distrust circled in her brain. After leaving for work the next two nights, she drove around the block to make sure the lights were off and he was not entertaining any guests.

A few days later, Ryan cornered her. "You know you're so damn paranoid! I didn't spend a dime on a package. Lou called me and wanted to get high. *He* paid for it, not me. What did you expect me to do, tell him no? You'd get high, too, if you got it for free."

"No, I would not. I would never do it without

you," she whimpered, a tear in her eye.

"Oh, yes you would, and you're only lying to yourself if you think you wouldn't."

"You're such an asshole!" she yelled, turning from him and searching for anything to throw at him.

"This isn't a one way street, you know!"

"Oh, yes it is!"

"Well, then, you're going the wrong way!"

"Fuck you!" she shouted as she picked up the wicker basket from the kitchen table and hurled it at his head.

He approached her with extreme caution, opened his arms, and hugged her tight. "Let's not argue. I'm sorry, but you have to understand how hard it is to refuse, especially when it's free." He kissed her hard on the lips. She nuzzled her head in his chest and wet his shirt with her tears.

The next morning, they awoke with the incident erased from their minds.

When Ryan returned to the office the following week, his brother-in-law and partner informed him about the financial difficulties concerning their landscaping business. "Ryan, we have clients who have not paid their bills in over two months. We can't even pay our own vendors."

"Really, that sucks," Ryan said, concerned.

"Yes, and I'm afraid it's getting so bad we can't afford to draw a paycheck," his brother-in-law said, disillusioned. "Well, I don't want to see it happen, but maybe we should just close up shop."

The business was close to ruination. They did not acquire new clients, and they lost a couple of their contracts. Ryan needed to borrow money, which he did not have to keep the business afloat. Over the next month, they closed their doors.

With Ryan broke and out of work, Amy started to smoke crack in the evenings before work. She took her last hit minutes before leaving the house and drove to the Milton Arms, jonesing for another hit. She began her shift high and trembled at her desk for an hour. She stained her paperwork with coffee rings, filed documents incorrectly, and grew very irritable. "Why can't you people do anything right?" she snapped at the chef and one of the chambermaids.

Ryan collected unemployment checks until his six months expired, and the bills continued to mount. They had no extra cash, and the crack nights dwindled to once or twice a week. He periodically borrowed more money from his brother and his mother. Sometimes he paid them back, other times Robert let it slide.

One afternoon Ryan stopped to visit his mother, who lived with his sister Patti and her husband. After about an hour, she noticed his dirty, torn sneakers.

"For God's sake, Ryan, why don't you buy some new sneakers? I thought I brought you up better than that," she asked, angry with him for his lack of pride in his own appearance.

"I know, Mum. A good pair of sneakers costs a hundred bucks or more, and I don't have that kind of money," Ryan explained, lowering his head shamefully. He knew she would open her pocketbook.

His mother reached down to the pocketbook on the floor beside her chair, opened her purse, and handed him two hundred dollars. "Take this and go buy some sneakers, and while you're at it, get a haircut."

"Gee, thanks. Mum. I appreciate it," he told her with a guilty grin. When he got into the car, he dialed Junior, who met him at the house with three packages.

Ryan got into the routine of deliberately inviting Lou to get high. He hoped he could get Lou to support their habit. He visited once a week and paid for an eight ball, but it still did not stop them from borrowing money from family or ignoring invitations to family gatherings. Amy began to receive letters from the bank and the Internal Revenue Service. She threw them away. The rent was now three months behind, which forced them to move before the landlord could evict them.

There was not enough cash for the first and last month's deposit on a new apartment. Amy made a telephone call to her friend Jill. She knew Jill had several friends, and maybe she knew about an empty apartment.

"Hello, Jill, how are things hanging?" Amy asked.

"Great. I still work at the Presidential, and I have a serious boyfriend. How are you doing?" she asked, sounding happier than she had the last time Amy talked to her.

"Things are good. I called to ask you if you know anyone who might have an apartment for rent."

"Wow! Did you read my mind, or what?" Jill squealed. "My friend Jason has a two-bedroom apartment in Medford. He lost his roommate two weeks ago. He needs someone to share it with him. Do you mind sharing?" she asked.

"It depends on how big it is. Any chance Ryan and I can take a look at it?"

"Yeah, sure, I can give you his number, and I'll call to let him know you're my good friends." She repeated his number to Amy twice to make sure she wrote it down correctly.

"Thanks, Jill. I'll call you soon, and we can get together for a drink."

"Goodbye, Amy, and please call me. I would love to see you and Ryan."

"I promise. So long, talk to you soon. Goodbye."

With no other recourse, Ryan and Amy shared the two-bedroom apartment with Jason, leaving the bills and bill-collectors behind. Amy placed most of their belongings in heated storage for safekeeping. The oversized apartment overlooked Princeton Street in Medford and had a huge bedroom with three windows. Jason allowed them to inhabit a small den for their private use, but they shared a living room, a kitchen and a bathroom. Ryan crammed their clothes into a cutout section of the wall in the den covered by a blue curtain.

Amy traveled back and forth across Boston in heavy traffic every night to get to work, which was not only time-consuming, but also inconvenient. She showed up late for work on more than one occasion. It was the last place on earth they expected to live, but they had no other options. Jason, a musician, spent most nights entertaining in nearby clubs—in fact he rarely spent time in the apartment, which gave Ryan and Amy free reign to get high there. They smoked crack five out of seven nights, and the stench of crack smoke began to permeate the apartment. It took six months for Jason to realize what was happening.

"Hey, you guys have to leave!" he said adamantly. "It's just not working out. I have other interested friends who need a room." He started to interview perspective roommates immediately, forcing Ryan and Amy to pack up quickly and get out.

Amy dissected the newspaper and scheduled four interviews for a new apartment. On the third day, they found two in West Quincy. By moving again, they managed to escape the bill collectors, and she stopped receiving letters from the Internal Revenue Service.

They rented an inexpensive one-bedroom in a large five-dwelling home next to a beautiful park. The new place consisted of three enormous rooms. The back door opened into an oversized kitchen with four cabinets above a Formica countertop. An eight-by-ten window sat above the kitchen sink, looking out over the park. Adjacent to the kitchen, Amy found a bathroom with tub. It was more than enough room for them. The threshold from the kitchen led to the living room with a large connecting bedroom.

The apartment walls were chipping paint, and every room needed to be painted and scoured with greased lightning. Heavy scrapes and slight gashes streaked across the kitchen floor. The rusted refrigerator and gas stove needed replacement. It did not resemble a Comfort Inn, but most of the repairs were fixable and the apartment would be a home.

"Don't worry Amy," Ryan told her. "I'll fix most of the problems. A can of paint will go a long way, and we can make it livable. It's not as if I'm working. I do have the time. I'll paint all the rooms, so just think about the colors you want," he told her.

"Oh, Ryan, that will be wonderful. It's a great idea. Thanks," she said.

He retrieved their belongings from the storage facility. Selling half of everything, including their beautiful butcher-block kitchen set, paid for a security deposit, repairs, and, of course, a few packages.

Desperate for a job, Ryan met with friends who worked on the Boston Central Artery Project, a.k.a. "The Big Dig." A good friend talked him into joining a local union, and he worked the night shift, two hundred feet under the ground. Ryan made three times the amount of money he had made with the landscaping business, and the bills disappeared. The job brought men and women laborers from all lifestyles. His use of cocaine became unbridled, and he began buying packages in the morning after work.

One day, as Ryan filled in on the day shift for a coworker, he directed the operator of a front-end loader to a bundle of piping. Realizing he had the wrong strap to lift the pipe, he told the operator he would be back in five minutes. As he made his way across the yard to the supply shack, backup alarms rang throughout the yard. He heard one alarm get louder and turned to look over his right shoulder to see the back of the front-end loader inches away. It was right on top of him. It struck him to the ground and catapulted him several feet forward. As he looked up, the machine was still traveling in his direction, and the eight-foot high wheels were just a foot away from him. He had no choice but to freeze and lay still. The mammoth machine passed over him, and several workers rushed to his aid.

Everyone, including Ryan, knew it was a miracle he was still alive. When the doctors examined him, he sustained only abdominal strain and bruises on his back. In hindsight, his reaction time saved his life. To this day, the incident remains a safety lesson used in union training classes. For months after the accident, the union veterans reminisced about how lucky Ryan was to survive that day.

Since Ryan and Amy now worked the night shift, the money poured in, and they partied almost every day after lunch and every weekend. They tried to sleep during the day after they finished the packages and rarely ate dinner. They mostly drove to Burger King or McDonald's before work and gulped the food down before getting out of the car. Spending close to a thousand dollars a week, they dug a tumultuous hole that eventually buried them.

On days when the sun bubbled like heated butter and the air lacked a summer breeze, Ryan sunbathed at the park while Amy slept. It became a benefit of working the night shift. One particular afternoon in

July while walking back from the park, he met someone.

"Good afternoon. How are you this lovely day?" Ryan said, waving his hand in friendship to an older woman who sat on her stoop. A smile came over her full, slightly wrinkled face. Her brown gaze looked beyond anything in this world, as though she wandered through a peaceful meadow picking daisies. The brownish gray strands of her hair stuck together, and she needed a cleansing shampoo. Bald spots between the clumped strands of gray shimmered in the sunlight. Grease spots stained her worn shirt and tattered slacks. She reeked of body odor and required a lengthy soak in a bubble bath.

"Hello, good morning. Are you the man who moved in the apartment across the street," she asked him.

"Yes. My name is Ryan," he answered, approaching her a little closer. "My wife, Amy and I, moved in a couple of months ago. What's your name?"

"I'm Mary Bennett. My mother left me this house, and I've lived here all my life. My husband Peter is from Braintree. Do you paint houses?"

Ryan found this a strange question to ask someone she had just met. He glanced at her curiously, "Well, yeah, I did in the past for friends and family. I just finished painting my apartment, but I don't do it on a regular basis. Why do you need a painter?"

"Are you from Quincy?" Mary asked, ignoring Ryan's question and turning her empty gaze in the direction to the park across the street.

"Yes. I have lived in Quincy all my life," he answered.

"Do you paint houses inside and out?" she asked with a seemingly one-track mind and lack of interest in Ryan's responses.

He looked at her strangely. "Yes, I do. Do you need a painter?"

"Is your wife from Quincy, too?"

By now he realized the woman suffered from some mental disorder. "No, my wife is from Medford. Do you need a painter?" he asked with an irritable undertone.

"Well. I need someone to paint my kitchen. What will you charge me?"

He softened his words and spoke compassionately, "I would have to look at the size of your kitchen and how much work I need to do. Then I can give you a price."

The woman stood and opened her door. "Come on in and take a look." She was a simple-minded woman who did not seem to care about allowing strangers in her home.

Ryan followed her cautiously into the hallway and took a long whiff. The house stank of body odor, cigarette smoke and dog urine. As he walked into the kitchen, he observed yellow-stained walls from grease splatters. The kitchen curtains, though blue and white in color, had a brown tint from years of grease and cigarette fumes. The kitchen ceilings and walls needed much more than a paint job, but he pitied the woman.

"I can probably paint the kitchen for three hundred dollars," he advised her.

"Okay," she said. "When can you start?"

Ryan laughed. "Let me talk to my wife, and I'll get back to you."

"Does your wife come from Quincy?" she asked, obviously forgetting his earlier responses.

"Yes," he lied. "I'd better leave now. I have to get home to my wife."

Returning to his apartment, Ryan found Amy sitting at the kitchen table, drinking her first cup of coffee. He described the details of his walk.

She laughed. "Are you really going to paint this crazy woman's kitchen?"

"Sure, why not? We can certainly use the extra money," he said, knowing half of it would go toward a package.

On Saturday, Ryan knocked on Mary's door. A peculiar-looking bald man around five feet tall with no teeth in his head answered. He wore a ragged, dirty T-shirt and stained denim jeans with no shoes or socks. His glassy eyes shimmered from an alcohol glaze and an obvious inability to fixate on anything in particular.

"You must be the man my wife met the other day. Come on in," he said, as he offered Ryan his outstretched palm and guided him down the hallway to the kitchen. "My name is Peter. We've lived here for twenty-five years. My wife tells me you're a painter."

Ryan laughed quietly under his breath, "Well I have done some painting in the past, and when I met your wife, she asked me to check out your kitchen. I told her I won't do it for less than three hundred dollars. I want to make sure you're happy with the price, and if so, I'll start Monday morning." He stared at the man, who was half his size and expressionless. He wondered if the man would speak again, but he never did.

"That will be fine," said a voice from behind Ryan. He glanced over his right shoulder and saw Mary standing at the threshold between the living room and the kitchen. "Have a seat," she urged, pointing to one of the kitchen chairs. Ryan pulled a chair from the table and sat next to Peter. "Monday will be good." She turned and glared at Peter. "This is my husband, Peter Bennett."

"Yes, we have already met," Ryan told her.

Peter went to the refrigerator and pulled out a beer for him and one extra. He turned to Ryan. "Want a beer?" he asked.

"Sure," Ryan said, reaching for one. For an hour he drank with Peter, who rambled on, leaving Ryan no opportunity to voice his opinion.

"This is a very quiet neighborhood," Peter said. "Nothing ever happens here. The guy next door owns a construction business, and his trucks come and go all day long. It's annoying. He's the nosiest person in the neighborhood. The people in the house next to him are Italian. They grow their own tomatoes, but be careful, 'cause they're nosy and unfriendly."

"This is all very nice to know," Ryan finally interjected. "Thanks for the info." As nutty as the

Bennett's seemed to be, he enjoyed their company. After three beers and a friendly conversation, he rose from his seat to leave. "So Monday morning will be okay?" he asked.

Peter glanced curiously at Mary, who answered for him, "Yes, it will be fine."

"Okay, I'll see you at eight."

* * *

The following Monday morning, Ryan toted his brushes, rollers and tarps across the street to Mary's open door and knocked. Hearing no response, he went in. Upon entering the kitchen, he found a young, attractive chestnut-haired woman sitting at the table with a cup of coffee.

"Hello, I'm Ryan," he said to her. "Is Mary here?"

"Yes, she's in the bedroom," the woman replied with dancing pecan-nut eyes. She bobbed her oval chin to a room behind the kitchen wall. "Hi, I'm Lindsay, a friend of Mary's." She stood and approached him with an outstretched hand. As they shook hands, Ryan avoided her gaze and looked around the room at the walls and the ceiling. He was more interested with the work at hand than he was in Lindsay.

"Nice to meet you. I'm here to paint the kitchen," he said straightforwardly. "This place really needs a great deal of work."

"Yes, it does, but they have no money. Mary told me you were coming. I come over every Monday morning to have coffee with her. She has no friends, and I feel bad for her. She's bipolar, you know."

"Oh. Now I see. I noticed something a little strange when I met her."

"Yes, she has some difficulty communicating with people, and her husband takes care of her the best way he can, but he's no brain surgeon either," she whispered, not wanting Mary to hear. "Would you like a cup of coffee?" She rose wobbly from her chair and placed her shaky fingers on the coffeepot handle.

"I would love a cup!" Ryan said, dropping his painting supplies on the kitchen floor and taking a seat at the table with Lindsay. She placed the coffee in front of him with a trembling hand. He glanced at her pale face and dishpan hands. He knew instinctively from experience she must have had a bad night. "So you seem a bit hung over. Tough night?" he asked her with a playful tone in his voice that ended with a chuckle. He blew on the hot coffee and took two slow sips as he stared at her, taking in everything he could about her. He waited patiently for a reply.

"Yeah, I was up most of the night. Do you party?"

"Yeah, my wife and I party sometimes."

Mary emerged from the bedroom. Lindsay pressed her forefinger against her wild cherry lips. "Shush, not in front of Mary. We will talk later."

Lindsay hung around and watched Ryan paint. Somewhere during the conversation, they instantly became friends. She had been forthcoming with all kinds of information for someone she hardly knew. "I have a twelve-year-old son who lives with my mother because I can't afford to take care of him," she confided in him. "He stays with me on the weekends. I don't work, and I get monthly welfare checks. Mary and Peter help me out occasionally, and my boyfriend gets me pills. I sell my food stamps for coke," she sighed, and spoke to him as though she knew him for years. "Do you smoke pot?" she finally asked.

"Yeah, of course," he said with not a hint of hesitation.

"Any chance you can get me a bag?"

"I'll call my friend right now." Ryan took his cell phone from his pants pocket and dialed. "Hey, Willy Boy," he said, grinning at Lindsay.

"Ry, what's up?" echoed the earpiece.

"I need a quarter-ounce. Can you hook me up?"

"Sure, when do you need it?" the voice bounced back.

"You tell me?" Ryan asked with an unpretentious demeanor.

"I can see you around three. Where do you want to meet?"

"How does Faxon Park sound?"

"Good, see you at three." Ryan closed his cell phone and placed it in his pocket. He leaned back in his chair, cupped his hands behind his head, and smiled at Lindsay, "You're all set. I'm meeting him across the street at Faxon Park around three."

Lindsay smiled back at Ryan. "That was quick," she told him, slumping down in her chair and relaxing her body in her thoughts.

"Willy can get anything I need—pot, coke, Percs [Percodan], and even 'H' [heroin] if you want," he said casually. "He's big into the H. Now let me start the painting, and I'll meet him when I'm done." He rose from the table after finishing his coffee and placed the painter's tarps on the appliances.

"Well, I have to go now," Lindsay said. "I'll see you around there?"

"No, you better make it three-thirty."

"Okay, see you then. 'Bye for now." She left the kitchen and headed for the front door.

After finishing the day's work, Ryan met Willy at the park and returned to Mary's house to give Lindsay her Baggie of pot. She paid him with food stamps.

It took Ryan three days to paint the kitchen. Around two on Thursday afternoon, Ryan appeared at Mary's door to grab his money. Under the circumstances, he was worried that Mary would not pay him.

Lindsay opened the front door. "Hi there. Mary went grocery shopping. I was low on cash and stopped by to sell her some food stamps. Come on in. She should be back any minute."

Ryan and Lindsay sat down at the kitchen table, drinking a Coors Light. "So any special plans for the weekend?" she asked.

"No, I think I'm just going to get high with the wife. Would you like to come by, maybe have some dinner, and get high with us?" he said with an encouraging smile. He had a habit of taking in lonely souls the way some take in stray cats.

Lindsay glanced at him. "Of course, I would, but I have no money," she said, turning her flushed face away in embarrassment.

Ryan smiled at her. "Don't worry about a thing. I have enough to get us high, and besides, Mary still needs to pay me for the paint job."

Lindsay smiled eagerly and nodded her head. "What time should I be there?"

A moment later, they heard the front door open. "Let's say tomorrow at six," he whispered to her with a snicker. He smiled, and they both began to laugh.

He rose from the kitchen table and walked toward the door. "Mary, do you need help with the groceries?"

"No, Peter just pulled in the driveway. He's helping." Mary dropped the bags on the floor with a thump and stored the groceries in the pantry. Peter entered the kitchen, dressed in his dirty hospital uniform, and placed the remaining bags on the kitchen table. He grabbed a beer, sat down at the table, and opened his first Michelob without changing his work clothes.

Ryan noticed the dirty soiled uniform and asked, "So Peter, where do you work?" He tried to overcome a twinge of disgust at him.

"I've worked in the kitchen at Quincy Hospital for thirty years. I graduated high school when I was twenty-one," he replied proudly.

Ryan stared at him strangely. "Twenty-one!"

"Yeah. Twenty-one. They kept me back a couple

of years."

Ryan scratched his head and snickered. "Sounds like more than a couple. Oh, well I don't think it's a good idea to brag about it."

Peter stared at Ryan with a non-compos glare and grabbed another beer from the refrigerator.

After about an hour, Ryan rose from the table to leave. "I need to get home for supper. Can I have my money now?"

Peter, now on his fourth beer, pulled his wallet from his back pocket and handed Ryan three hundred dollars. Ryan turned to Lindsay and smiled. "See you tomorrow?"

Peter and Mary stared at them with crooked eyebrows. Ryan saw their puzzled stare and interjected, "I invited Lindsay to come for dinner and meet my wife." The Bennett's looked at one another and lowered their heads in silence.

Ryan walked across the street and rushed through his apartment door. "Hey Amy," he shouted. "I invited a friend for dinner tomorrow."

Amy appeared from the bedroom. "What?" she said, frowning in anger and disbelief. "I don't have enough food to feed another mouth." She prepared meals with enthusiasm, but disliked cooking for unexpected guests.

"Don't sweat it. Peter paid me for the painting, and their friend gave me fifty dollars in food stamps. We'll order a couple of pizzas."

"So who the hell did you invite to dinner?"

"I met a cool woman over Peter and Mary's. She likes to get high, too, so I invited her for dinner, and we can get a couple of packages for later."

The next evening around five o'clock, he picked up the phone, ordered two mushroom pizzas, and dialed Junior. He spent all of his paint-job money and gave Amy the food stamps.

"Gee, thanks, you're a good shit," Amy said sarcastically. "What, no cash?"

"Well, do you want to get high or not? How the hell do you expect me to pay for it, with my good looks?" Amy walked away and said nothing.

Junior arrived at five-thirty, the pizza delivery boy arrived at five-forty, and Lindsay knocked at six.

The moment this short, attractive woman with a white translucent blouse and black miniskirt up to her ass entered their lives, the mood began to change. Amy smiled half-heartily, not caring to show her disapproval of the woman's appearance. She threw a sharp glance in Lindsay's direction as her body trembled for no apparent reason.

"Come on in and meet my wife," Ryan gestured with a stimulating smile. The strange woman slid provocatively in the doorway like a soft breeze before a rainstorm. Ryan turned to Amy. "Baby, this is Lindsay."

"Hello. Nice to meet you," Lindsay said, her smile beaming from earring to earring.

Amy smiled. "Hello. Won't you have a seat?" She pointed to the kitchen table. "I hope you like pizza. The pizza guy just delivered," she said, not looking at the new woman as she placed the forks, knives and paper plates on the table.

"Yeah, sure, no problem," Lindsay replied,

smiling as she planted a wet kiss on Ryan's lips. Amy frowned, and Ryan recognized her look of disgust. He had an awful habit of kissing and flirting with women— one she disliked, but had gotten used to over ten years of marriage. She took a deep breath and let out a sigh, showing her irritability. She dismissed his actions, knowing she had no control over his flirtatious nature.

Ryan approached her, kissed her hard on the lips, and whispered in her ear, "Stop it. You need to relax. She's just a friend. I love you!" He kissed her again on the cheek.

He made a vodka and cranberry for Amy and handed Lindsay a Coors Light. He grabbed a beer for himself and sat down at the kitchen table. Opening the first box of pizza, he placed two slices in each of the three plates.

Amy stared at him in surprise. "I thought you didn't like to eat before you got high."

"I know, just one piece to be sociable." He smiled at her culpably. She gave him a dirty look and took a bite of her pizza.

Sitting at the kitchen table, they finished off one pizza. They drank, chatted about Lindsay's situation, and laughed about the neighbors. Lindsay barely seemed to notice Amy and directed most of her conversation toward Ryan.

She explained the Bennett's behavior. "They are mentally slow. Some would say mentally challenged, but they function at a higher level. Peter and Mary are extremely independent but rigid. They stick to a set schedule and never waver for a moment."

To Amy's amazement, Ryan ate all three slices of pizza, and while he sat listening to Lindsay, he started to make a pipe. After the girls had finished eating, Amy picked up the second pizza and placed it on top of the microwave.

Ryan pushed himself away from the table and walked to the stove to cook the coke.

Lindsay continued her rhetoric. "Peter gets up Monday through Friday at three in the morning. He gets dressed, drives to work, and makes his coffee while he works. He has done this for thirty years, exactly at the same time and in the same way."

Meanwhile, Ryan moved to the stainless-steel sink and finished the cooking. He placed the crack rock on a plate. Lindsay and Amy heard a "ting" sound as the rock hit the plate. In anticipation of getting high, they began to gag as they moved to the living room.

Lindsay continued her narrative as she walked to the living room, taking a comfortable seat on the couch. "Mary takes the dog out every morning at nine o'clock. She makes her breakfast and watches TV until Peter comes home at two in the afternoon. The only day she leaves the house is on Friday to go grocery shopping."

"Wow, I don't believe I have known anyone so methodical," Amy chimed in with curiosity. She thought of everyone she knew. She stared back at Lindsay and thought of how much she reminded her of the Chatty Cathy doll she had as a child. *The woman never shuts up,* she thought.

"Yeah, believe me. You can set your watch to

their schedule," Lindsay remarked assertively

Ryan brought the plate of crack in the living room and set it on the coffee table. Amy and Lindsay watched the new movie *Jackass* with Johnny Knoxville while Ryan set up the first hit. Amy studied Lindsay, taking in everything she could about her. Lindsay babbled on in a loud, annoying caterwaul. Amy prayed for a hit just to keep her quiet. Her clothes were bargain-basement, her lipstick cherry-red, and her short brown hair appeared tousled by the evening's windy breeze. Her eyes sat deeply in their sockets. She painted her nails candied-apple-red, and her hands were paler than most, making their blue veins more prominent. She squirmed nervously in her seat, making Amy uncomfortable.

"You seem nervous. What's the matter?" Amy asked. "You act as if you're afraid the police are about to break down the door." Lindsay smiled, saying nothing. "Are you okay?"

"Oh, yes. I'm fine. I just can't wait for a whack, I guess."

Regretting her first impression, Amy began to warm up to Lindsay over the course of the evening. "So, do you get high often?" she probed, this time with a genuine smile.

"My boyfriend Tommy does coke and pills too, but he works the evening shift," Lindsay explained with ease. "On his nights off, we usually get high. I don't get to spend a lot of time with him."

"It must suck being alone in the evening..." Ryan cut her off. "Hey, you can always come here for dinner whenever you get lonely. We don't mind the company," he said as he set up the first hit. Amy threw him a discouraging glance.

"Thanks for the invitation. I don't want to intrude, and I manage to get out when I can," Lindsay replied with a warm and nervous laugh. "I was psyched when Ryan invited me over to meet you. It's cool to make another female friend. I have real bad anxiety attacks and can't work. I don't meet too many people, and I like to thank you again for inviting me. I get government assistance and food stamps from the government. If you're ever short on cash, I can always buy you food with my stamps."

Ryan handed the loaded pipe to Lindsay, who sucked in her first hit.

"Oh, no, it's okay. Right now we don't need anything. We're fine," Amy said, regretful that Lindsay must stoop to such measures. "I have not met the Bennett's yet. How long have you known them?"

Lindsay handed the pipe back to Ryan, who loaded Amy's hit.

"I met Mary about two years ago," Lindsay said, coughing from the smoke. "Although they've been simple-minded people, I've been very nice and generous. Mary is crazy. She consistently suffers from mood swings. One minute she's talking a blue streak and not making any sense, other times she gets depressed and won't talk. I like them and try to help when I can."

Amy took her hit and handed the pipe back to Ryan. He sucked long and hard, choking as he exhaled.

As the conversation exhausted itself, the three of them finished watching the movie.

Lindsay turned to Ryan with glassy eyes. "It is so nice of you guys to get me high and stay for dinner. I promise to give you some food stamps. You can get some lobsters or a nice piece of steak." Ryan handed her the pipe once more.

As he continued to pass the pipe back and forth, the girls wavered through short dialogue, dead stares, and TV while he glared at the walls. The three of them bonded, and the crack party lasted well into the early morning hours.

Once they finished, Ryan and Lindsay smoked a joint. Amy made a rum and Coke. After several minutes, Lindsay walked the short distance home. Ryan invited her to get high with them once or twice a week. From then on, she ate dinner with them every Friday evening, and on the nights they smoked crack she slept over instead of walking home by herself at such a late hour.

The pain in Amy's lower back continued to throb annoyingly, so she hired Lindsay two days a week to clean the bathroom and kitchen floors for fifty dollars. Later Amy regretted her snobbish attitude and decided to help with the cleaning.

One morning, Amy woke with a nasty hangover.

"I'm so pissed you bought those packages last night!" she complained to her husband. "Now we're broke and short on food!"

Ryan laughed. "What the hell is your problem? I didn't hear you say no when I passed you the pipe."

"You suck!" she squealed. "I hate you!"

He laughed at her again. "Grow up. You're never happy. We never fool around anymore. When was the last time you sucked my dick? How do you think I feel? If you don't like it, then leave. No one's stopping you, especially me."

She ran into the bedroom crying and slammed the door behind her. Ryan sat on the couch just laughing and shaking his head.

On one of Ryan's Thursday afternoon walks through the park, he noticed Lindsay lounging on an overgrown patch of green grass with a young man. He wore a white tank top and frayed blue jeans and had a shaved head, which shimmered in the sun. Ryan approached slowly, his eyes narrowed, his lips pursed in disapproval, and his chin tilted defensively. Looking directly at Lindsay and ignoring the man with her, he said, "Good afternoon. How are you this beautiful day?"

Lindsay pushed her palms in the grass and lifted herself up. "Hey, Ryan. Good to see you. I'm glad you stopped." She hugged him tightly. "I'd like you to meet my boyfriend, Tommy." She turned toward Tommy as he lifted himself off the grass.

Ryan extended his hand to Tommy, "Hi, nice to meet you. I'm Ryan."

"Likewise," Tommy replied, blasé, with a strong grip and tug of his hand. He returned to his shaded dimple mark in the grass as his eyes followed Ryan curiously.

Ryan ignored Tommy and turned to Lindsay, "Are you all set for tomorrow night?"

"Yeah, sure, same time?" she asked with a grin like a cat scoring the cream.

"It sounds good to me. I have to get back now. See you tomorrow." Ryan turned to Tommy and nodded his head. "It was nice to have met you."

Tommy simply nodded back, "Likewise." Ryan turned his back on them and walked the short distance home. He decided he did not like Tommy. There was something odd about him, but he could not put his finger on it.

The next night Lindsay knocked at the O'Connors' door for dinner. During their second hit, they heard a loud knock at the apartment door. Everyone froze with a silent stare. Ryan jammed the pipe and the coke plate under the bed. He walked cautiously to the kitchen window and peeped through one of the Venetian slats. He stepped back from the window as two more knocks smacked the door. He turned his eyes to the bedroom threshold and stared at Lindsay. "It's your friend, Tommy," he whispered.

"You're shitting me," she whispered back. "He must have gotten out of work early."

"Shush. I'm not letting him in. I don't have enough for him. No one move until he leaves."

A few minutes later, Tommy began to yell, "Lindsay, I know you're in there! Open the door!" The apartment remained quiet. Tommy stealthily walked along the side of the house, peering in the windows. Everyone inside the apartment stood like Roman statues and remained as quiet as a whispering blade of grass through the summer breeze. Tommy moved to the sidewalk and glared up at the apartment windows. "Let me in!" he yelled once more. After no response from the apartment, he turned and stomped off in anger.

Ryan approached the window and peeked through once again. Tommy was gone. He approached Lindsay. "I don't want him here," he told her flatly.

"I'm sorry," she said despairingly. "He must have followed me, or something."

"Next time I'll pick you up, so he doesn't follow you," Ryan insisted.

He ignored Tommy over the next week, and eventually Tommy stopped following Lindsay. From then on Ryan picked her up at the end of the street on Friday nights. Lindsay began to cool her relationship with Tommy, and as the weeks passed, he disappeared. Ryan found out later the police had arrested him on possession charges.

After a month of dinners and weekend highs, Ryan, Amy and Lindsay sat in the living room on a careless Friday night. As the exhilarating crack rush overtook Ryan's total being, he rose from his chair. He smiled down at them with lust and anticipation. He peered at Lindsay. "I like getting naked when I get high," he told her. "Do you mind if I drop trou?"

She laughed unashamedly. "No, not at all. Whatever you want to do is fine with me."

He began to undress. He gently undid his buttons and opened his shirt to expose the short, curly blond hairs on his chest. He slid the shirt off his shoulders and let it drop to the floor as he flexed his pectoral muscles. He unbuckled his belt and stepped out of his jeans. He stood naked in front of the girls.

They stared up at him, and their lips tightened. Their faces flushed a light shade of pink from the rising warmth fueling their bodies.

"Come on, girls, get naked with me," he prodded them.

The girls glanced at each other and shrugged their shoulders in a "why not" manner. Lindsay smiled at Amy and removed her blouse and her skirt, revealing a matching set of black panties and bra. "Come on, Amy, your turn," she urged.

Amy stood and pulled her shirt over her head. She did not hesitate to get naked in front of another woman. She found it exhilarating, and it was not as though it was her first time.

Lindsay grinned with feral delight. She faced Amy, grabbed the waist of her pants, and slipped them down over her full, round hips. The pants slid to the floor, exposing Amy in red satin panties.

Ryan picked up the coke plate from the coffee table and retreated to the bedroom. "Come with me, girls, and we'll do another hit."

The girls reached the bedroom, stood naked in front of the dresser bureau, and smoked. As the crack rush surged through Ryan, he massaged Amy's pussy with the first two fingers of his right hand. He placed his left palm over Lindsay's right breast, squeezing and fondling it until her nipple hardened. As her cheeks blushed, he bent over and suckled each nipple one at time.

With a lustful appetite Lindsay stepped forward

and took Ryan's penis in hand. He grunted in pleasure and slowly lifted his head as she stroked his cock faster in her palm.

Ryan rubbed and pressed his thumb hard against Amy's clit as she moaned loudly. His body tensed as he fondled and sucked on his playmates. Though crucially close to *ménage a trios'*, his body craved another hit, and his dick wilted.

After the next hit, he commanded Amy, "Now get on the bed on your stomach." A slow smile came to his lips, and his chest rose in and out as he breathed deeply.

Amy got on the bed and laid facedown.

Lindsay smirked with an untamed pleasure and sat on the bed. "Go ahead, Lindsay," Ryan commanded her. She spread her legs wide and shoved her clit into Amy's face. Amy pushed her tongue in Lindsay's pubes and spread her lips apart with long, slow licks. She licked deeper and lower, sliding her tongue in her wet center. As Lindsay moaned in pleasure, Amy sensed Ryan behind her as his soft cock slid into her buttocks. He pumped it slowly, back and forth. She gasped for breath. "Keep sucking," he told her. He poked the head of his penis around her dark crinkled ring, but he was too soft to enter her. He began his in-and-out rhythm, sliding up and down from her vagina to her dark ring. He continued to pump Amy's buttocks as she licked Lindsay to orgasm. Lindsay screeched out as the explosive pleasure shuddered through her body. She pulled her wet pussy away from Amy's lips.

Amy never went down on a woman, and as the

crack rush diminished, the white skin of her freckled face turned a bright red.

Ryan smiled down at them as his lips tightened, and his cheeks glowed with delight. "I think it's time for another hit."

After smoking the entire package, Lindsay had to meet her son early the next morning, and she walked home. Ryan and Amy rolled into bed around two in the morning.

Heather McCarthy

NEIGHBORS

The following weekend, the new neighbors invited Ryan, Amy and Lindsay for dinner. Everything Ryan and Lindsay had said about them rang true.

Mary had an unkempt appearance and wore grease-stained clothing. Her hair was shoulder-length with clumps of gray streaks, and her chin drooped over a sagging neck. She kept silent over the evening and never spoke unless someone asked her a question.

Peter, despite sixty years of age, looked ten years older, and shaped his head in a crew cut. His scalp was a dark shade of brown from the lack of a shower. His toothless jowls left him with an over-closed mouth and sunken-in cheeks. He weighed about ninety pounds, and, God forbid, he looked close to death. He lacked coherent intelligence and common sense.

Ryan and Amy brought potato salad, and Lindsay made onion dip. The group sat at the dining-room table, drinking beer and eating Ruffles potato chips smeared with dip. Amy picked up her drink and noticed a water-ring on the tablecloth. She took her napkin and wiped the water away. When she turned the napkin over, she noticed the black streak of dirt. It made her stomach turn sour, and she wanted to vomit. She looked at Ryan and whispered, "Look, isn't this disgusting?"

Ryan shook his head and said nothing. He did not want to embarrass anyone.

Everything seemed serene until Peter scooped the onion dip onto his potato chip and licked the dip off with his tongue. He dipped the tip of the chip back in the dip. Lindsay glared at Amy and turned to Peter.

"Yuck, Peter!" she cried loudly. "That is so disgusting. What's the matter with you? We all have to eat my dip. You're gross!" She pushed the dip in front of him. "Here, you finish it. We don't want anymore."

"Fine with me," Peter said, deaf to his boorish manners. "It's a pretty good dip, and it just means more for me."

Mary prepared an undercooked pork loin with green beans and a disgusting German bread stuffing for dinner. Ryan and Amy ate bits and pieces, leaving the raw portions of pork on their plates. Amy helped to clear the dishes from the table and placed them into an already soiled sink with grime and greasy dried pots. Lindsay scrubbed down the table with Lysol. Amy watched in disgust as Mary scraped the plates of uneaten food into a plastic-lined wastebasket, rinsed the dishes with soapless water, and placed them in a strainer to dry.

Amy turned to Ryan. "Since I have to work tonight, I think maybe it's time we should leave."

Ryan glared at her with a questioning stare. "I thought you were off tonight."

"I got a call earlier. The hotel wants me to do some overtime. You do remember?" She winked at him with her left eye.

"Oh yeah, right, sorry, I forgot." He rose from his seat. "Well, thanks for dinner, but we have to go. Amy has to work." Lindsay and Amy followed him to the door, expressing their thanks and regrets to their hosts. The three left immediately, returning to the apartment for another night of hitting the pipe.

Ryan and Amy never ate at Mary's home again, but Amy did invite Mary and Peter to the apartment for dinner and associated with them only through short friendly encounters, out of sympathy for them.

Ryan and Amy continued to get high with Lindsay regularly, but not always with sexual overtones. Lindsay never paid for the product and agonized about the money. She tried to give them food stamps, but they always declined.

The next Thursday evening, Lindsay knocked at the door. "Hey, guys, I have a hundred dollars. Let's get high," she said, pushing her way into the apartment as if it were her own. She lowered her head, keeping her eyes away from Amy's face, as she smiled at Ryan and kissed him on the cheek.

Ryan dialed Junior, but the phone just kept ringing. He turned and dialed Nokie.

"He'll be here in an hour," Ryan told the girls. Then his smile faded. "Lindsay, where did you get the money?" he asked her in an irritated voice.

"I borrowed it from Mary," she told him,

grinning from cheek to cheek. "They have plenty. Mary keeps a cigar box full of cash in a hope chest in her bedroom. There must be at least three thousand dollars in it."

"Really, wow. You have no money. How the hell will you pay her back?"

"Oh, it's easy. I'll pay her back in food stamps. I get three hundred dollars' worth every month, and I never use all of them."

"Well, just don't get yourself in trouble. You still have to eat, and remember, if you fall short of stamps, you can always have dinner with us."

After two more phone calls from Ryan, Nokie finally knocked an hour later, and Ryan bought six packages from him. After Ryan cooked the coke, they had only twelve hits instead of thirty, because Nokie had added B12 to the coke—otherwise known as "cutting it" in order to make more money. Ryan phoned him immediately.

"What the fuck, Nokie? The stuff you gave me came back like shit. I want three more!"

"No, man, I can't. I'll give you extra next time."

"If you don't come back now and give me more, I won't call you next time."

No, man, I can't," Nokie repeated, and hung up.

Ryan clenched his brow and wrinkled his nose as he glanced at Amy and Lindsay. "What the fuck? I'll call Junior." He lifted the receiver and dialed. "We'll smoke what we have until he gets here."

They smoked the twelve hits in an hour. Junior arrived after their last hit, and Ryan bought another six packages. And again, after Ryan cooked the packages, the results were the same. "This stuff sucks!" he hollered. "Let's finish this, and I'll try to clean the pipe."

After they had taken their remaining hits, Ryan grabbed a pair of scissors and cut the plastic bottle in half. He scraped the resin from the bottom and sides with the scissors, leaving a dark brown residue on the plate. It yielded another three hits each. He taped the bottle back together and made a new hole for a straw. The hit from the residue was twice as potent, and from that moment on Amy always made Ryan clean the pipe.

By the time they finished, around four in the morning, Ryan did not want Lindsay walking home alone, so she spent the night on the couch.

Late the following morning, Lindsay left after drinking her coffee, and Amy sank into the couch and watched a movie on Turner Network Television while Ryan remained in bed, flipping through sports channels.

Later in the evening, Ryan told Amy, "I'm going to invite Lou to party with us, because we have no cash and I know he wants to get high. He'll be happy to pay."

Lindsay arrived ten minutes before Lou. She handed Ryan a hundred.

"Where did you get this money?" he demanded.

"I borrowed some more from Mary," she told him with a guilty smile.

They heard another knock at the door. Lou squeezed through it cautiously and handed Ryan his cash. Ryan looked at Lindsay. "Hey Lou, I'd like you to meet my friend, Lindsay."

They nodded their heads, smiled at one another, and shook hands. Lou liked what he saw. She was sexy, and he could not wait to get high with her.

"Hello, how are you? It's very nice to meet you," Lou said first.

"Hi," Lindsay said with a silly giggle. "It's nice to meet you, too."

Junior arrived fifteen minutes later. As he opened the door, Ryan turned to Lindsay. "I would like you to meet my friend, Junior."

"Hello," Lindsay said as she shook hands with him. Once he completed the introductions, Ryan paid Junior the sum of three hundred dollars, including a hundred of his own money. He closed and locked the door after Junior left. He walked to the kitchen sink, prepared the coke, and cooked it on the stove while the others sat jonesing on the couch. When he finished, they followed Ryan into the bedroom.

Lou took the pipe and set up his hit. After smoking, he returned the pipe to the top of the dresser. Ryan snatched it up and prepared a hit for Lindsay. As she exhaled, she handed the pipe back to Ryan, and he set up a hit for Amy. After the girls smoked, they moved to the living room. Lindsay sat on the couch, picked up the remote, and flicked through the TV stations while Amy logged on to Pogo.com. Ryan called from the bedroom ten minutes later, "Ready, girls?" They loved the sound of those two tiny words, because it meant it was time for another whack.

When the girls entered the bedroom, Lou stared

at them with a horny smirk. "Why don't you girls take off your clothes?" he prodded eagerly. They shook their heads, did a hit, and walked out, ignoring him.

"Amy, can you show me how to play those computer games?" Lindsay asked.

"Yes, have a seat at the desk." Amy stood over her shoulder and showed her how to play. Lindsay was a quick study. She played with the computer while Amy spread a deck of cards on the coffee table and played Free Cell.

Every ten minutes the girls returned to the bedroom for another hit, then retired to the living-room couch for more TV and games. Suddenly, Amy turned to Lindsay/ "So where did you really get the cash?"

"I took it from Mary's cigar box. They have so much. She'll never miss it." Amy glared at her in disgust and turned her face to the TV without another word. After a few seconds, Amy went to the kitchen to make a drink, when she heard Ryan shout, "Ready!"

The night continued in the same fashion, and the four finished the packages at three in the morning. Ryan made everyone a cocktail. After they guzzled that down, Lou left, and Lindsay crashed on the couch.

At eleven the next morning, Amy woke to a loud, hard knocking at the door. She rose, lightheaded and nauseous. In her bare feet she shuffled to the kitchen door and opened it a crack. Mary stood there with a full-sized paper bag. She pushed her shoulder hard on the door and forced her way into the kitchen.

"Where is Lindsay?" she yelled.

"She's not here," Amy spoke softly. "She left last night."

"Well, this is her junk. I'm leaving it here. I do not want that bitch in my house again. She's not welcome ever again."

"What's the matter, Mary? Why are you so upset?"

"She stole a hundred dollars from me!"

"Oh, Mary, I find that hard to believe," said Amy in a consoling tone.

"Don't tell me she didn't," she argued in a voice loud enough to wake the dead. "I counted the money last night, and now this morning I found a hundred dollars missing. She was the only person in my house since yesterday morning. I know she did it. Tell that bitch not to set foot in my house again." Mary dropped the bag on the floor and abruptly walked away.

Lindsay heard the yelling and rose from the couch. She made her way to the kitchen with sleepy eyes as Amy shut the door. "What the hell was that all about?" she asked, giddy with a sour stomach from her crack hangover.

"Mary left your things here. She doesn't want you in her house again. She knows you stole the money."

"How the hell did she know? I always took a few bucks here and there, and she never said a word."

"She counted it. She knows," Amy said disgustedly. She feared their association might have caused Lindsay to steal, and she did not want be part of such treachery.

Lindsay sighed in despair. "I guess that friendship is over. Oh well, I'll try to fix it another day, when I don't feel so shitty." She glanced guiltily at Amy. "Do you mind if I make a pot of coffee?"

"No, not at all. I think we can all use a cup of coffee. When Ryan gets up, he'll make us some breakfast."

Lindsay dressed in her clothes from the previous night. She went to the bathroom, washed her face, and combed her hair. All the noise had woken Ryan, and he headed to the kitchen to start breakfast. Their hangovers kept them all silent through breakfast.

After Lindsay had finished a second cup of coffee, she rose from the table. "I think I'd better leave now. I have to see my son today."

"Okay, see you tomorrow?" Ryan asked.

"Yeah sure, it sounds like a plan."

She was rushing to the kitchen door when Amy stopped her. "Mary is sitting outside on her stoop," Amy said. "It may be a good idea to leave through the front door. She must be watching the door. I don't think you want to run into her right now."

"Yeah, that is probably a good idea, thanks. Goodbye, see you later." Lindsay picked up her purse and walked out the front door.

The foursome partied at least once a week, and sometimes more. A month after Lou met Lindsay, he decided he wanted to do more hits with them. Whenever the girls entered the bedroom, he said, "Why don't you girls take off your clothes?" They always shook their heads, did a hit, and walked out, ignoring him.

"He's so weird," Lindsay said one day. "He has drool all down his jaw. It's disgusting."

"Oh, that's just Lou," Amy reassured her. "He gets horny when he smokes, but don't worry, he can't get it up anyway."

"Whatever, but I still don't like him." The girls giggled and took a seat on the couch.

Another ten minutes passed. Ryan hollered again from the bedroom, "Ready?"

This time when the girls entered, Ryan and Lou were standing nude in front of the bedroom bureau. "Come on, girls, Ryan and I are naked," quirked Lou. "What about you?"

"Take off your tops, at least so we can see your tits," Ryan encouraged them patiently.

Lindsay and Amy smoked their hits, ignoring the boys' remarks. "Come on, girls," they insisted unanimously.

"Take those tops off," Lou beckoned.

As her euphoric head-rush and sexual awareness overtook her, Lindsay pulled her tank top over her head, revealing her young, firm breasts and chocolate nipples. She giggled and glanced at Amy.

"Oh, what the hell," Amy said, and removed her Boston Bruins T-shirt. The boys gleamed from ear to ear with lust as the girls left for the living room. Ten minutes later, Ryan hollered to them for another hit.

Amy entered the living room just as Lindsay rose from the couch. The girls walked side by side into the bedroom. "Come on, girls, take the rest of your clothes off," An impatient scowl flooded his face as he pleaded with them. Ryan shook his head in agreement.

The girls lowered their eyes, shunning their advances, and smoked another hit. Once the exhilarating rush overcame Lindsay, she pulled her sweats down and slid her red lace panties over her slender hips. She glanced at Amy and laughed sensuously. Amy dropped her pants. She wore no panties. The four of them stood, naked, smoking another hit. Amy placed one arm in front of her tits and covered her pussy with the other hand. Feeling uncomfortable in front of Lou, she left the room, leaving Lindsay behind. Amy had learned over the years that crack makes normal individuals do things they otherwise would not.

After what seemed a long time and jonesing for another hit, Amy walked into the bedroom before Ryan had a chance to call her. She found Lindsay stroking Lou's penis. Lindsay was visibly embarrassed, having just said she disliked Lou. "I don't get it," she announced. "I guess it must be the coke."

"Hey, baby, come stroke my cock," Ryan urged her in a sultry command. She walked to the bureau, smoked another hit, and began stroking Ryan's penis slowly, up and down. Ryan only concentrated on the next hit instead of Amy's hand on his cock. He went limp once again. She did another hit and left the room, uninterested in any more group foreplay. When she returned for her next hit, she found Lindsay stroking Ryan's penis while Lou stood, masturbating. She frowned annoyingly and left the bedroom again after finishing her hit. The rest of the night, she remained in the living room and returned to the bedroom only for her hits. She did not like the three of them together in the bedroom, but had no desire to join them.

As Amy played computer games, Ryan and Lou played with Lindsay. As Ryan readied the pipe and lighter for his hit, he urged Lindsay, "Okay, baby, suck it." The sensation of the coke rush and Lindsay's lips around his cock were second to none. She sucked up and down slowly until it was time for another hit. When she finished her next one, she turned to Lou and began to suck slowly on him. They finished the packages at three in the morning. They all drank a cocktail. Lou left, and Lindsay slept another night on Amy's couch.

Over the next few days, Ryan kept company with Lindsay at her apartment while Amy slept. One afternoon, Amy woke up early to find Ryan missing. Her curiosity got the better of her, and she stuck her head out the kitchen window, which overlooked the park and Lindsay's apartment. She was not the type who would spy on her husband, but when it concerned another woman, it was a different story.

When Ryan returned later in the day, Amy was waiting for him in the kitchen. "Where the hell have you been?" she asked him in a loud, angry tone.

"I had a drink with Lindsay. Why? What's the big deal?"

"I do not want you to spend time with her. I want you to stay away from her. I know she's after you."

"Oh, don't be ridiculous. You're so jealous. Stop it."

"I mean it, Ryan. I do not like her."

"I'll do what I want!" he said firmly. "You can't tell me who I can and cannot see!" She was scared now. She had never seen him so angry.

"I do not want her in this house again!" she screamed, her face deepening with disdain.

Ryan laughed sarcastically. "You really think I'm going to listen to you?" He laughed again. "This is my house, too, and I'll invite anyone I choose!"

"We will see about that," she scowled.

Three days later when Lindsay came to clean the house, Amy fired her. "And don't bother to show up for dinner!" she said angrily. "I'm not a restaurant!"

Now Ryan and Amy argued daily, and the coke came back like crap. It turned an oily shade of brown as he cooked it, and the return was only half the usual amount. The price of their habit doubled, along with their debt. They bought packages nightly in an effort to get high, but the results were always the same. With their credit cards maxed out and their paychecks gone, their cravings intensified along with their arrears.

One night while waiting for a delivery, Amy turned to Ryan and asked him, "What do you want for dinner?"

"Are you fucking stupid, or what?" he shouted. "You know I don't eat before getting high. How fucking long is it going to take you to figure it out?"

A tear flowed down her cheek, "I'm sorry!" she said, fraught with anguish. "What the fuck is your problem? I only asked a simple question."

"Yeah and a stupid one at that!" he growled.

"Fuck you, too!" she screamed. "I suppose you're going to call the whore down the street, too."

"Why not? She gives better head than you do."

"Oh, I see," she said sarcastically. "Then maybe you should fuck *her* instead of me. That is, if you can get it up."

A knock pounded on the door. "Get the door. Your coke whore is here," she snapped, with tears in her eyes.

Ryan opened the door. Lindsay entered, and Amy stared at her in a cold "I'm going to get you" look. "What the fuck do you want?" she screamed. "Did you come to blow my husband's brains out, you fucking whore?"

Lindsay stepped back from her and grinned at Ryan like an evil siren. Amy wondered whether all men were so naïve and insensitive, or whether it just happened to be her bad luck.

Ryan stepped between them, blocking their views of one another. He faced Amy. "Where the hell are your manners? Look at you! You're the one acting like a nut! Why the hell are you talking to her like that? She didn't do anything to you!"

"Oh, no, don't you dare talk to me about manners! You could learn a thing or two," she hollered, alerting the entire apartment building to another O'Connor fighting spree. "Oh, no, she didn't do anything except try and steal my husband from me. She's just a fucking coke whore. She wants you."

Amy turned to the kitchen table and picked up a box of Cheez-Its. In one swift motion she hurled it at Lindsay, missing her head by mere inches, and it slammed into the kitchen door with a loud thump.

Ryan grabbed Amy firmly by the arm. "Are you fucking crazy? What the fuck is the matter with you?"

"Get the fuck out, and take your coke whore with you," Amy screamed.

"Let's get out of here," he said turning to Lindsay. "We'll go to your house and have a beer."

"Good, get the fuck out!" Amy shouted.

"Fuck you!" he yelled as he walked out with Lindsay and slammed the door behind them.

Amy sat at the kitchen table, blubbering. The longer she mulled it over, the angrier she became. She got up from the table, put on her shoes and ran to her car. She drove to Lindsay's house and ran up the stairs to the door. Lindsay answered with a beer in her hand.

"Where the fuck is my husband!" she hollered, pushing herself through the doorway. She stomped through Lindsay's apartment and checked each room. She found Ryan sitting at the kitchen table.

"I want you to get home right now!" she demanded.

"Fuck you! You need to go home and cool off!"

Amy grabbed Ryan forcibly by the arm. He pushed her softly away. "Get away from me!" he shouted with red flames in his eyes. He knew she had no right to be angry. He made no secret of his relationship with Lindsay.

Amy hesitated and stepped back from him, looking as though he had just slapped her. She turned from him and pushed Lindsay. "You fucking whore! You're not getting my husband!"

Lindsay slapped her across the face, and Amy punched Lindsay in the stomach. The girls scratched at each other with long, sharp nails and yanked hard at one another's hair. Ryan jumped from his chair and placed his arms between them. He grabbed Amy and hauled her down the stairs and out to the car. Once the rage of her Irish temper ceased, he leaned on the passenger side door. "Now, what are we going to do?" he scolded.

She rubbed her eyes and blew her nose. "I want you to take me home," she said, looking in his face with contempt.

Ryan moved away from the car and opened the door. "Get in." He drove her home, not saying a word, while she sat in the passenger seat and balled her eyes out.

When they arrived home and pulled in the driveway, Ryan turned the car motor off and walked into the apartment, leaving the front door wide open. Amy sat in the car, mulling over what to do next. Ryan appeared at the open door. "Are you coming in, or can I shut the door?" he said sternly. "I'm not leaving the door open all day."

"Yes, I'm coming," Amy said sadly. She walked up the porch steps and passed him in the entryway. "You're such an asshole," she said with a look of contempt as she continued into the bedroom.

"What the fuck were you thinking?" he asked as

she stomped away from him. "Why did you do that to Lindsay?"

"I hate her, and I want you to stay away from her," she said, turning once more to give him a threatening stare.

"Well, I can't do that. She's my friend," he told her plainly. "Go take a nap. We'll talk later after you cool off."

Their arguing continued for days, and Amy begged Ryan to get rid of Lindsay, but he continued to stay friendly with her. He spent a few afternoons a week drinking with her while Amy rested for her night shift.

Amy finally took action. On a blistering Sunday in August, she awoke early and packed a bag. She waited for Ryan to leave the apartment and slipped out, taking whatever she could carry. As the sky unbolted with a roar and the rain pounded on the windshield, she drove to the nearest motel and checked herself into the room. Before she inserted the key in the lock, the whites of her eyes streaked beet-red, and her cheeks were wet from tears. She walked into a typical dingy motel room and threw her suitcase on the bed by the door. The wallpaper hung slightly away from the walls and showed signs of peeling in all four corners. She threw the car keys on the flimsy table by the window and turned on the television. The air in the room held the smell of mildew, which seemed to emanate from the bathroom. In her rain-drenched clothing, she dropped face down on the bed and cried herself to sleep.

Around two in the afternoon, she slowly rolled over on her back and opened her eyes, not recognizing where she was. The room air smelled of mold, and the sun shining through the picture window temporarily blinded her. She grew increasingly tired, even though she had slept soundly—tired of the pain and watching her world change. She placed her feet on the faded carpet floor, undressed, and took a shower. The rust-stained showerhead no longer gleamed, and it was five minutes before the water ran hot. After showering, she sat on the unmade bed and stared unseeingly at the TV. She examined the room in a thoughtless gaze, already feeling lonely and despondent. She believed dealing with another woman was entirely different from dealing with Ryan and his addiction. She sensed her husband slipping away, with no idea of how to save her marriage.

She left the tiny room at ten in the evening for her eleven o'clock shift at the hotel and stopped for breakfast each morning at Bickford's Restaurant next door. Other than work and meals, she never left the hotel room. During the afternoon hours, she cried herself to sleep or watched idiotic shows bursting forth from the flat-screen TV.

As the feelings of loneliness, paranoia and body-shakes from drug withdrawal became too much for her to handle, she packed her bag. Ignoring the problem was the not the way to solve it, so she drove home. In no mood to fight, she quietly entered the apartment and softly placed her overnight bag on the kitchen floor.

"Is that you, Amy?" Ryan called pensively from the living room.

"Yes." She stood in the doorway and said nothing more.

Ryan rushed to her side. He smiled warmly down at her, and when she smiled back at him, he kissed her lips and hugged her tight. He let her go, and as he pushed her from his chest he said, "You look like you need a package." With her lips still pouted, she shook her head yes. As much as she hated the idea of buying another package, her body craved another hit. It had been four days, and she was jonesing. She knew it would be impossible to stop.

Three days after returning home, Ryan and Amy bought a few more packages. As soon as she satisfied her body with a toxic level of crack, they were in love again. With the incident forgotten, they went about their daily routine. They fought briefly about his relationship with Lindsay, and she begged him to get rid of her.

After a month, Lindsay slowly disappeared from their lives.

Two years later, Lindsay Dwyer died in bed from an apparent overdose.

WIGGING OUT

Over the next several months, their habits remained the same. Ryan and Amy continued to get high, borrowing money from family and friends, ignoring the bills, and taking cash advances on their credit cards. Amy applied for new credit cards as soon as the old ones maxed out. Ryan bailed out on numerous family outings, including weddings and baby showers. Their relatives stopped sending invitations.

Amy invited the Bennett's over for dinner several times. She did not intend to return to their house for dinner. Ryan maintained the Bennett's lawn in the summer and shoveled their driveway in the winter. The couples helped one another through bad times, as good neighbors should, and the Bennett's always had money to lend. Ryan borrowed at least a hundred dollars a week from them, and eventually paid them back within a week or two after Amy and he received their paychecks.

One Friday morning, after finishing a night shift, George Mills summoned Amy to his office. "Amy, please have a seat. We need to talk." He sat behind his polished antique desk and frowned. He wore an air of discontentment, and Amy had never had the privilege of seeing him that way. She knew he was annoyed, but did not know why. She rolled her eyes and grinned.

She took a seat in the chair directly in front of his desk, crossed her legs, and primly placed her hands in her lap. She slowly swung her free leg back and forth anxiously. "What can I do for you, Mr. Mills?" she asked with a shaky voice and glazed eyes.

"Amy, you have done a wonderful job as night manager. I could not have done a better job if I had done it myself, but you have changed." He leaned into his desk and opened a manila folder. "In the last year, you have called in sick eleven times, came in late twenty-three, and have lost your temper on dozens of occasions." Mr. Mills sat back in his chair and placed his hands behind his head. "I need you to understand my position. I cannot have my managers disregard hotel policies and allow them to remain employed. You're setting a bad example for your subordinates." He leaned his elbows on the desk and intertwined his hands over the manila folder. "I like you very much, and I would like to help you, so whatever the problem may be, you need to fix it. I am going to give you some time to come to grips with whatever it is you need. That is the reason I must let you go. I hope you will use this time wisely and straighten out whatever is bothering you. I am truly sorry. I had your last check drawn up this morning." He stood, leaned over the desk, and handed her an envelope.

Amy stood with tears in her eyes and took the envelope. She could hardly blame him, considering the facts he placed before her. "I'm sorry, too. I hoped you would have been a little more understanding."

Mr. Mills closed his eyes and slowly turned his head side to side. "I'm sorry Amy, but there is nothing I can do. I like you very much and have grown close to you over the last several months. I hope things work out for you." He came out from behind his desk, walked her to the door, and extended his hand. "Maybe in the future, if things work out we can look at hiring you back. Thank you for coming in, and goodbye."

Amy, with tears flowing down her cheeks, shook his hand and left. She drove home, dripping tears on the steering wheel.

She arrived home around eight-thirty in the morning. She noticed Ryan's car in the driveway. "Oh, shit, what will I tell Ryan?" she whispered to herself.

She walked into the apartment and found Ryan preparing breakfast.

"Good morning, pretty lady," he said. "Are you ready for breakfast?" He turned and, seeing her red, watery eyes, asked, "What's the matter, are you okay? Did you get in an accident? What's wrong?"

"Oh, Ryan," she wept softly, a single tear at first, followed by a gusher. "I got fired."

He stood tall over her. She buried her head in his chest, and he hugged her tight. "Don't worry about it. We will get by," he promised. "It's not your fault.

We've been partying too much. Maybe it's time we laid off for a while." He took her by the shoulders and pushed her away from his chest. He looked in her eyes. "Look at me," he said. She raised her head and, through moist eyes, gazed into Ryan's warm, compassionate face. "We'll lay off the shit, and let's just be thankful I still have a job. Everything will be fine, trust me."

"Okay, but no more partying. Right," she begged him. They hugged once more. Amy took a shower and went to bed. She slept until three in the afternoon.

The next week flew by with no crack, but when the weekend arrived, Ryan wanted to party. Amy had no job to worry her, and their minds told them they needed to get high. They were "on a roll" again, and Amy spent her days cleaning house and watching TV instead of looking for a job.

Ryan arrived home at seven-thirty the following Friday morning. He walked into the apartment and found Amy still sleeping. He moved to the bed. He placed his hand on her shoulder and shook her awake. "Hey, get up," he insisted. "I got us a couple of packages from work. Hurry up and get up."

Amy rose, blurry-eyed and yawning. "What the fuck, Ryan. It's too early," she stammered.

"Come on, get up. Once you're up, you'll feel fine. Let's go."

They spent the morning getting high and slept until dinnertime, but ate no dinner. Ryan dialed Nokie at six. "Hey, man, I need four," he told him.

Amy glared at him, "We have no money left.

How the hell are we going to get anything?"

"Relax. I'll get him to cuff me."

"He didn't do it last time. What makes you think he'll do it now?"

"He will. Trust me."

Nokie knocked at seven, and Ryan asked for three. "I thought you needed four?" he asked.

"The last three I bought were crap, so you owe me. Give me three, and we'll call it even."

"No, man I can't." Nokie hurried to the door as Ryan barricaded it with his body. "Man, stop it! Let me out!" he pleaded.

"You're not leaving here until I get those packages. You owe me," Ryan demanded, beet-red in the face and with blazing fire for eyes.

With no recourse, Nokie relinquished three packages and slammed the door on his way out.

Saturday night, Ryan called Nokie again. "You got money this time?" he asked.

"Yeah, I got money. How long?"

"You sure, man?"

"Yeah, I'm sure."

"An hour," Nokie told him.

"Ryan, what the hell are you doing?" Amy asked, exasperated. "He'll never give it to you after last night."

"Give me a check," Ryan ordered.

"No more checks. You bounced five checks this month, and the bank is threatening to close my account."

"Just give me a check and hurry up. If you're so damn worried, I'll give it back to you when I get paid," he demanded with wide glaring eyes and narrow lips.

Amy handed him her checkbook, and in a flash he left to cash a check at Stop & Shop. He returned with milk and bread, just in time to meet Nokie at the door.

Ryan prepared to cook the coke, and Amy followed closely in his footsteps. "Why are you bird-dogging me? Go sit down," he said, blocking her view with his body.

"I think it's about time I learn how to cook this shit. I want to watch," she said, glaring at him with tightened lips and a clenched jaw.

"Okay, I get the picture, but don't get too close. If you bump me and this goes down the sink, we're fucked."

All of her anger left her body, and she relaxed. She watched closely as Ryan poured the white powder in a spoon. He added half the amount of baking soda. He turned the faucet to a slow dribble and filled the spoon to the top. He unfolded a paper clip and, using the end, mixed the three ingredients together to form a smooth white liquid. He carefully carried a spoon to the stove. He turned the gas burner to medium-high and placed a spoon over the flame. He gradually mixed the ingredients with the end of the paper clip until the mixture began to bubble. Just before it appeared to bubble over, he slightly raised the spoon from the flame. He continued to cook the spoon until all of the baking soda dissipated and the coke settled to the bottom. He returned to the sink, added a smidgen of cold water to cool the concoction, and poured off all of the remaining water. With the end of the paper clip he slid the wet crack to the plate and let it dry to a hard rock.

"So that's how you did it," she remarked with a smile. "It's like baking." She laughed.

"Yep, that's how it's done," he replied with a sigh. "It came back like shit again. Looks like maybe five hits each. Right now, the stuff out there sucks."

They moved to the bedroom and stripped. They each smoked their hits, and as the rush filled their heads, Ryan turned to Amy. "Lay down on the bed."

Amy smiled fervidly and lay on the bed.

"Now spread your legs," he commanded coyly. She did so without hesitation. "I want you to play with yourself. I want to watch you come."

Amy grinned shamefully. She spread her legs and placed two fingers on her clit. She rubbed it as her chest rose and collapsed in gasping breaths. Ryan placed his hand around his cock and stroked it as he watched Amy climax.

She rose from the bed and smoked another. The crack tasted like shit and smelled like rotting garbage. The high lasted two seconds, but they finished their five hits each, made a cocktail, and went to bed early.

It was not long before Amy started to cook and smoke her own packages when Ryan was not around. Her addiction grew stronger, along with her inability to pay the bills.

She woke up early Monday morning to the telephone's earsplitting ring. She got out of bed, holding her head in her hands, and picked up the receiver.

"Hello?" she said, staring out the living room window.

"Hello, Good morning. May I speak to Mrs. O'Connor, please?"

"This is she. Who am I speaking with?"

"Mrs. O'Connor, this is the account manager from the Credit Union." His irritating voice was curt, but professional.

"Yes, what can I do for you?" she replied in the same manner.

"I'm calling this morning to advise you on a bank decision concerning your account. I'm afraid we must close your checking account. You'll still be able to use your savings account."

"Why? I don't understand," Amy inquired, looking a bit grimmer than when she had picked up the phone.

"The bank made the decision on the grounds that you have had thirty-five checks returned for insufficient funds over the last six months."

"You must be joking. My account was with your bank for the last fifteen years. How can you do this?"

"I'm sorry, but the amount of checks returned is far above normal. I realize you have been a customer with us for a very long time, and it is the reason we are allowing you to keep your savings account. Again, I'm sorry."

"I know I bounced a lot of checks, but I paid the fees. Whatever, if you close my checking, then you can close my savings too," she replied sarcastically, hoping he would change his mind.

"It is entirely up to you. If you like you can stop by the bank sometime today," he told her, not reacting the way she expected.

"Fine," she told him, hanging up the receiver with a smash. She sat on the couch with a pouty look and a tear in her eye.

Ryan heard the smash of the telephone, and from the bed he yelled, "What's the matter? Who was on the telephone?"

"The bank just closed my checking account!" she yelled back.

"Fuck, oh well. Suppose things could be worse. We'll just open another one somewhere else," he chuckled. "Not to worry. What's for breakfast?"

"I don't know. I don't feel like cooking. Shall we get an egg sandwich at Dunkin' Donuts?"

They had both gained a considerable amount of weight by now. Eating junk food had become a way of life for them, but it was easier not to cook when they suffered from crack hangovers. However, fast-food restaurants contributed to the demise of Ryan's health, and he put on over a hundred pounds. Amy gained a smaller amount of weight, but she was more self-conscious about her appearance. It surprised her, because most crackheads typically weighed less than two hundred pounds. She considered it a blessing in disguise, because it helped them hide their addiction from friends and family.

"Yeah, let me get up, get dressed, and I'll go," he told her.

Ryan drove behind the woman at the automatic teller machine and waited for her to finish her transaction. As she grabbed her receipt and card from the slots, he shifted into drive. The woman did not move. He hollered at the windshield, "What the fuck, lady! Come on, move it!" Through her rear windshield he saw her fussing with her pocketbook and papers. He yelled again, "Why the fuck can't people have the courtesy to move up and sort their papers out so the next person in line can get to the machine?" She eventually moved, and Ryan pulled up to the ATM.

An hour later he returned to the apartment, opened the door, threw his car keys on the table, and screeched out one word, "Fuck!"

"What the hell is wrong with you, and what took you so long?" Amy hollered from the living room. "I'm starving!"

"And you think *I'm* not?" he bellowed in anger. "I tried to buy the sandwiches with an ATM withdrawal from the credit card, and they denied it. I couldn't get any breakfast. I have no cash. You'll have to cook. This is really starting out to be a shit day."

"Okay, okay, calm down. How about some pancakes?"

"Anything. I'm hungry."

Amy rose from the couch, entered the kitchen, opened the refrigerator, and removed the eggs and the Aunt Jemima maple syrup. She opened the cabinet above the refrigerator and took out a box of Hungry Jack pancake mix. While she prepared breakfast, Ryan picked up the television remote. He did the "man thing" like most men and flicked rapidly through the channels. She never figured out why men did such things. "Why can't they just take the time and look at the on-screen guide and choose what they want to watch?" she whispered so he could not hear her.

Amy set the table, and ten minutes later she called Ryan. "Okay, breakfast is ready!" He entered the kitchen, wearing sweatpants but no shirt. She moved close to him and snuggled her face in his neck. "You smell good enough to eat."

"Yeah, yeah, let's eat." He hugged her tight and kissed the top of her head. "Don't worry, we'll figure this all out," he said as he cut his pancakes with the knife. As he picked up his fork, he said, "You know, you need to find a job, and soon, because my job on the 'Big Dig' is almost over. We both can't be out of work."

"I know. I promise I'll start looking tomorrow." Amy turned her head and looked shamefully away. They finished breakfast and did the dishes together, laughing. Their stomachs were full, and the day seemed brighter somehow.

Later the same day, Amy retrieved the mail and the envelopes of overdue bills from the mailbox. She threw the grocery circulars in the wastebasket and flipped through the envelopes. She found a letter marked important in big black letters from the Internal Revenue Service. With her hands shaking and her mouth open wide, she tore open the envelope along its left side. She read the letter slowly. The IRS demanded a four-thousand-dollar payment, threatening confiscate any and all property. If she did not pay within seven days, the IRS would take her wages.

Even Amy realized she must find a job, any job. She stood at the window, daydreaming. It started to snow. She watched it accumulate on the sidewalks. Her heart began to stir. She found it difficult to believe she had fallen so far. It was too hard to get out from under the hole they had dug, but worth a try. She began to see herself trapped in a life steadily unraveling with no way out. It had all been so perfect in the beginning, and she wanted to go back to those days, but knew the past would not rewrite itself.

It seemed incredible that they owed so much money to the government. She showed the letter to Ryan. "Just throw it in the trash," he said.

"How can I do that? It says they want the money in seven days," she reminded him.

"Trust me, they won't do anything. Besides, we don't have any money. You know the old saying, 'You can't get blood from a stone,' " he told her firmly. "We do not own anything of value. What can they possibly take?"

"I heard they could come in the apartment and take all our furniture."

"Amy, be realistic. The furniture is too old and of no value. They wouldn't want it."

Amy trusted him and threw the letter in the trash. It was the last she heard from the Internal Revenue Service, at least for a while.

On Tuesday morning, she started to look for a job. She got up early, showered, and chose a basic navy blue suit. She tied her long hair in a chignon and applied her makeup meticulously. She stopped suddenly to glance in the mirror for one last peek and, realizing how stunning she looked, she smiled. As she opened the door to her car, she slid into the driver's seat, feeling confident. She dropped off twenty resumes and made three appointments for interviews.

Her last meeting was a success. The employer invited her to his office immediately. She acquired a position at the Oceania Hotel as night manager. The money was the same as the Milton Arms, but it was ten minutes closer to the apartment.

After two weeks, she settled in at her new job. They got high only on weekends. Amy wanted to make a conscious effort to slow down.

Ryan received a call from a childhood friend five days after Thanksgiving. He and his wife invited them for a long weekend getaway at their condominium in Stowe, Vermont. With both of them working and money coming in, it seemed like an excellent idea. She was not required to work weekends at the Oceania Hotel until she finished her probation period. Vermont had plenty of snow this year, and it would be great to rent ski gear when they got there, or maybe a snowmobile if they had enough money. Amy was glad to be getting out of Quincy, and she wanted to share some quality time with Ryan.

As Amy removed the suitcases from storage and placed them in the bedroom, Ryan sat on the bed and enlightened her about his childhood friend. "Bill and his wife Heather are in the same dilemma," he said cautiously.

Amy glanced at him inquisitively and asked, "What do you mean?"

"They are functioning drug addicts. Bill and Heather are not your typical crackheads. They work hard and play harder. Like us, they don't rob others for their habit, but only rob themselves. They have good jobs, no kids, and have enough money to do exactly as they please."

Amy had difficulty enduring her disappointment. She began to wonder if Ryan knew anyone who did not do drugs, but she wanted to get away from a monotonous existence and have fun. She made the decision to go no matter what.

Amy showed him a carefree smile and asked, "What do they do for work?"

"Bill owns a security company, and Heather works in a hospital. I think she's a nurse. She's a good shit, and I'm sure you'll like her. She's just like you—very down to earth."

"Is she pretty?" Amy asked.

"Not as pretty as you," he told her with a cocky smile.

Amy grinned sarcastically, "Boy, you're such a charmer. Okay, now get out of here and let me finish packing."

Ryan stepped off the bed and headed toward the door. With an afterthought he turned back to Amy. "By the way, Bill wants me to bring up three eight balls for the weekend." He left the room before Amy had a chance for rebuttal. She knew he would never listen to her anyway. She sighed and angrily packed the remaining clothes, throwing them into the suitcase without folding them.

On Wednesday afternoon, Ryan ordered the three eight balls from Junior, who delivered them an hour after dinner. He smiled at Amy. "What do you say we do a couple of hits now?"

"I guess so, but give me some to hide, so we don't smoke it all."

"That sounds like a good idea. I'll split it up and repackage it for later. Now remember what I said. Don't give me anymore," he told her firmly.

When they finished smoking half of the three eight balls, Ryan pleaded with Amy to give him the rest. After fifteen minutes of his prodding and begging, Amy grabbed the other package from her hiding place. "Only take a small amount," she commanded. "Remember, you promised your friends, and we have to leave early in the morning."

"Yeah, yeah, okay," he replied, annoyed at her coddling.

Amy hid the remaining product. After finishing what they had, he begged her again. This time Amy remained headstrong and demanded that they go to bed.

It started to snow as they packed the car, but they carefully made it to Route 93 north. Ryan hid the leftover package in his suitcase, and it was not much, maybe one night's worth of partying. Fighting a crack hangover, they made their way through Massachusetts and into New Hampshire. The snow began to collect on the highway, making it slippery.

After two hours on the road, they stopped at the

Ninety-Nine Restaurant in White River Junction on the Vermont border to have lunch. Ryan slid into the booth next to Amy and ordered Chicken Caesar wraps with onion rings. As they waited for their order, he placed his palms on the table and stared at his wife. She knew instantly what he wanted. She placed her hands in his palms. "I love you, you know that," he said.

"Yes, and I love you too," she replied with a warm smile.

"You know this shit sucks," he told her. "I'm so glad you made me stop last night. It's so fucking addictive. I would have finished all of it if you hadn't stopped me."

"I know," she said, hoping he might someday find the courage to stop permanently. "For once I'm glad I had the strength to say no."

Ryan looked at her sorrowfully. "Even in the face of obvious despair, we still continue to try to live a normal life, and all the time being shackled to the devil. Let's face it—we couldn't even spend a little time away from home without letting the crack ruin a perfectly good weekend."

"I know," she said. "I want to stop, but I cannot resist the urges. Maybe we should try to stop. We should think about some outside help. Maybe we should go to meetings or something."

"Let's enjoy the weekend and talk about it when we get home," he told her with a tone of ennui in his voice as he took another bite of his sandwich.

She saw his look of indifference and dropped the subject. "How far are we from the Condo?"

"It's a little over an hour, and the snow is getting heavier, so we should get going. I'll pay the bill. Go have a cigarette, and I'll meet you at the car."

Ryan drove onto Interstate 89, headed toward the town of Stowe. He turned to Amy and asked, "How about a beana [his slang term for a blowjob]?"

She threw him a disgusted look. "I don't think so," she told him.

"Oh, come on. Go down on it. Right here, right now. It will be fun. A nice beana while I'm driving. It would be awesome."

"Oh, my," she said, shooting him a questioning glance. "Such a romantic nature you have, my dear. How could any woman refuse an offer as tempting as that?" she said sarcastically. "No thanks, I think I'll take a rain check. Besides, the snow is coming down harder, and the roads are too slippery."

He smiled at her and turned his eyes and thoughts back to the road. In a playful mood he began to sing a stupid little jingle, *"I've got a penis in my pocket. When I wake, it looks just like a rocket. Now and then, when you grab my stem, here comes another swollen rocket."*

Amy coughed to cover her laugh. She did not want to encourage him further. "Will you stop singing that stupid song, you fucking nutcase?" She laughed as she stroked her tousled hair, pulled it back from her cheekbones, and tied it in a ponytail. She smiled warmly at Ryan and turned back to the window to gaze out at the exquisite scenery.

As the falling snow swirled over the highway and lightly covered the New England birch trees, it made them think of Christmas and grand goose dinners—the kind they usually serve at old Yankee bed-and-breakfasts. They smiled at each other and began to sing Christmas carols. One song in particular Ryan loved to sing was "The Christmas Song" by Nat King Cole, and he sang it beautifully.

He drove north through the town of Barre, and while he kept his eyes on the road, Amy gazed out the window, taking in the beautiful scenery of lush farm-studded valleys covered in snow. She reminisced about her childhood and the times her father took her skiing. Life was somehow easier in those days. If only she could go back and start over—but life does not offer us those opportunities.

They drove steadily without stopping and reached the condominium in an hour and a half. The snow stopped temporarily, and the view of the clear blue sky hovering over the mountain astounded them.

Bill and Heather left the front door ajar in anticipation of their arrival. Five mailboxes lined the beginning of a long walkway. The condominium connected several townhouses to the left and back of the building. They rented a beautiful, luxurious two-story unit with a full dine-in kitchen. Beautiful oak beams lined the cathedral ceiling and ran from wall to wall, complementing a rustic floor-to-ceiling Fieldstone fireplace.

Ryan made all the introductions, and Amy happily relaxed. She accepted their friendship instantly and looked forward to an enjoyable weekend. She liked Bill but fell in love with Heather.

Ryan and Amy settled into one of the three bedrooms. After they had unpacked, Heather gave Amy the grand tour of the unit while Ryan enjoyed a cocktail with Bill.

"What a great condo you rented," Amy said.

"Thanks. Our friend let us have it for cheap money. Because it has three bedrooms, Bill thought it would be a nice idea to invite you and Ryan."

"I'm so glad you did. It will be a lot of fun."

The couples settled in a comfortable seat next to a blazing fireplace while it began to snow again. After they discussed plans for dinner, Ryan blurted out, "I have some good news and some bad. I only have two grams. Fucking Junior came by, and he only had four grams. I told him I needed four more, but he said he needed to meet his connection and would have more in an hour. So knowing he would be back later, we started getting high. I called him every half hour, but he never answered his phone. By this point, we dipped into two grams."

"What the fuck are you telling me, you only brought two grams?" Bill said, raising his voice in anger and disappointment.

"Look, he told me he was coming back! I would have brought what we agreed upon, because ninety percent of the time he comes back. I knew I'd replace what we smoked. It's not my fault he didn't come back! What the fuck you want from me? Of all people, *you* should understand. You're lucky I have any on me at all," he concluded with a guilty laugh.

Bill knew Ryan had lied, but what could he do? Ryan thought about their fucking addiction, knowing every day the hole was getting deeper and deeper.

After Bill had calmed down, they went to dinner at the Fox Fire Inn at the bottom of the mountain for Italian fare. The couples returned to the condo for their first whack off the pipe and a friendly game of dominoes. The girls teamed up against the boys and won. The past sexual experiences weighed heavily on Amy's mind, and she refused to repeat her prior indiscretions with this couple. It was more than Amy could handle, and she knew from Ryan that Heather would not have agreed to it because of the difficult life she had lived.

They talked for hours about work, skiing, and mutual friends. They rotated hits off the pipe, and the all-too-familiar "chase was on." They passed around the pipe until they depleted the packages and started to jones. Ryan cleaned the pipe to get back another two hits each. Bill made cocktails. They retired to their rooms, and Ryan and Amy rolled into bed some time after midnight.

The next morning, the four ate a late breakfast and headed to the mountain for a sled ride in rented tubes. The snow fell lightly, adding a wintry mix to the fun. That night they ordered pizza, listened to some tunes, and smoked a couple of bones "marijuana."

The next day, after an early breakfast, they all bought half-day ski tickets. At noontime, they headed down the mountain to the ski lodge for coffee with Sambuca and a Reuben sandwich.

Because Ryan and Amy were suffering from their usual crack hangover, they decided to drive the long ride home. He turned the radio up loudly, listened to the awesome sound of Carlos Santana, and they smiled at each other as the car passed over the Massachusetts border. When they reached the apartment, they dropped the suitcases on the floor and took a nap.

When Ryan awoke, he called Junior and received no answer. He called Dennis to find out if he heard from him.

"Who are you calling?" Amy shouted from the bedroom.

"Shut up!" he snapped callously. "I'll tell you later!"

Amy lay in bed, ignoring his irritability as she tried to listen to his conversation without much success. She knew the tone of a typical crack withdrawal. He always spoke that way when he needed another whack. When Ryan hung up, she asked, "What was that all about?"

"Hold on!" he yelled once again. "I have to call Bill!" He dialed another number as Amy continued to eavesdrop. "Hey, brother, called to let you know the cops arrested Junior, and that's why he never called me back." There was a silence as Ryan listened to his friend. Amy quickly stepped out of bed and grabbed her bathrobe. She entered the living room, and throwing the bathrobe around her body, she sat on the couch beside Ryan. She stared at him with a concerned look.

As Ryan hung up, she asked, "What happened?"

"Dennis told me the cops pinched Junior." He began to laugh.

"What the hell is so funny?" she wondered, concerned if the police had been watching them, too, and how long it would be before they broke down the door.

"It couldn't be any better. I lied to Bill, and now it turns out it wasn't a lie after all." Ryan laughed hard again.

"You're nuts," she said. "What'll we do about Junior? Do you think we should be worried about the cops?"

"No, but we'll lay low and deal with Willy. We can have him over for dinner to make it look legit." Amy lowered her face and said nothing. Ryan dealt with Willy for the next several months, because they learned from friends that Junior went to jail for two years.

A month after their Vermont trip, Ryan came home early from work. He angrily threw his lunchbox and dirty jacket on the kitchen floor.

"What's the matter?" she asked.

"I told you the job was almost over. The company laid off thirty guys this morning, including me."

"Damn, we never seem to get a break!" she said, looking desperate.

"Don't worry. I can collect unemployment for six months, and we'll be fine," he reassured her with a confident smile.

Amy continued to work the night shift at the Oceania while Ryan remained home, looking for work. By the time Christmas rolled around, their circumstances had deteriorated. They ate Christmas dinner alone, penniless, with no decorations or exchange of gifts.

BURIED

She hotel industry thrived through the holidays. After long hours of hard work and covering extra weekend shifts, Amy's boss rewarded her with a week's vacation after New Year's.

Ryan woke up early the day after Christmas, feeling energetic. He shaved, showered, and dressed. He grabbed the grocery list from the refrigerator, which Amy had started the day before, and drove to Shaw's Supermarket. It took him an hour to stroll down the aisles and find everything on the list. He waited almost half an hour in the cash register line and watched the woman in front of him flip through the popular tabloid magazines. *Why can't women be more like men?* he asked himself. *Do they all have to read that stupid shit, and do they truly believe what they read?*

Once he paid the cashier, he swiftly grabbed the bundles and carried them to his car with a troubled gaze. As he unlocked the door and threw the bundles in the back seat, he drove home, thinking about the overdue bills. He pulled into the driveway with a contented smile.

When he rushed through the door of the apartment like an excited child with a secret, he found Amy making coffee and frying the bacon. He placed the shopping bags on the kitchen counter and began to unpack them.

"I just had a brainstorm while I was shopping," he said. He noticed her nod as though she understood him, but she said nothing. In a few short minutes, she stopped preparing breakfast and quietly helped him place the groceries in the cupboards.

Ryan stared at her, waiting for a response. "Did you hear what I said?" he asked, irritated she might be ignoring him.

"Yes, dear, I heard you, she replied casually. "What idea do you have this time?" She thought about all the ideas he came up with during their long years of marriage, most of which got them deeper into trouble.

"I have fifteen thousand in the retirement fund from the union. It's not a huge amount of money, and there doesn't seem to be any reason to keep it in the bank. I thought we might cash it in to pay the bills."

She glared at him, and a pink flush covered her freckled cheeks. "Ryan, listen to me! I don't think it's a good idea," she said boldly and with some degree of conviction. "We'll need that money someday, and today is not the day." The last thing she wanted to do was get deeper in debt.

"It's my money. I busted my ass to earn that money, and I'm going to take it out. Once we have it, you'll feel different."

"It seems you've made up your mind—do what you want. You always do, but I think it's a bad idea."

"You're right. I'll do what I think is best." He hoofed it into the living room, grabbed the remote, and sat watching TV while Amy prepared the French toast. As he clicked the remote numerous times, all of the channels turned into a noisy black. "What the hell is going on!" he hollered into the kitchen to Amy as she placed the maple syrup on the table and arranged the dishes.

She heard his exasperation and walked in the living room. "What's wrong?"

"What's up with this fucking cable?" he roared.

She looked at the black snowy screen. "It looks like they shut off the cable TV."

"Do you see what I mean now?" he said. "We need that money. I'm sick of being broke. Is breakfast ready?" he barked with a look of disgust.

Staring down at their plates, they ate breakfast without a word. Ryan sliced his French toast into small pieces and squeezed the maple syrup over them. After a long, intense, deathlike silence, Amy spoke. "All right, if you want to take the money out, go ahead. I won't stop you." She kept her head down and frowned into her plate.

He gazed at her with a sparkle in his eyes. "Thank you! You do see how badly we need it, don't you?" he told her triumphantly.

"Yes," she said simply, picking up the dishes from the table. She washed the dishes and cleaned the kitchen. She stepped in the shower and consoled herself as the pulsating water pummeled her backside. After showering, she dressed in her favorite footie pajamas and grabbed another cup of coffee. They had no money left, and none of the dealers they tried to reach called back. Tensions were high, and they spent the day in separate rooms. Ryan watched TV in the living room, and Amy took a nap on the couch. They barely spoke to one another and ate lunch at different times. When Ryan finally rolled into bed around midnight, Amy quietly stepped out of bed and spent the night on the couch.

The next morning, Ryan awoke early and headed to the union hall, dressed in fleece sweats and a black sweatshirt. The lack of work and sitting around the house had gained him another hundred pounds; his dark shirt and roomy sweats made him appear thinner. He was out of shape, suffered from high blood pressure, and began to breathe heavily.

He got out of his car, placed his car keys in his pocket, and walked to the front door of the union hall, which was in a newly renovated building just outside Quincy Center on the corner of Copeland and Common Street. Entering the reception area, he gazed at the fifteen men waiting to find employment for a day or even a week. They sat on four wooden benches against the walls with looks of despair. He knew how lucky he was that Amy had an excellent job.

As he stepped closer to the union representative's office door, he grinned with pleasure when he saw his good friend Larry sitting behind the desk. "Ryan, how are you? It's been a long time," Larry said with a welcoming smile.

"Hey, Larry, what's up. How are you?" Ryan stood in the doorway of a dingy, cold room with wood-paneled walls and no windows. Larry had been a friend for years, and Ryan reminisced about the times he had spent with Larry and his wife and their two children before marrying Amy.

"I can't complain. Come in," Larry motioned to him with a sweep of his hand. "Come in, have a seat."

Ryan took the comfortable chair directly in front of Larry's desk. "I'm okay, but I'm short on cash. I came to see if I could cash in my annuity."

"Are you serious?" Larry looked startled as he watched Ryan nod his head disparagingly. "I understand. I guess I cannot blame you," Larry replied, looking completely sympathetic. "The situation is desperate. Everyone is looking for work since the Boston project ended. I only have one job available, and I have to choose one of the fifteen guys sitting outside my office."

Ryan shook his head and told him, "There's no work anywhere. I've looked for weeks."

"Yes, I've heard. I'm sorry you need to cash in your annuity. Okay, I'm sure I don't have to tell you it would be better to wait," he warned.

Ryan shook his head in agreement. He knew Larry was thinking only of his friend's well being, but Ryan had no choice.

"There are forms you must fill out," he said as he opened the file cabinet behind his desk and handed Ryan five sheets of paperwork. "Fill out the forms and I'll get the ball rolling. I might be able to get the corporate office to send out a check by Friday."

"Great, man, thanks." Ryan placed the

paperwork down on Larry's desk and filled out all of the required information. Larry returned to his mound of paperwork.

"So, how have you been? Have there been any issues from the accident with the front loader?"

Ryan looked up from the paperwork and smiled. "No, man. Everything is great. I went back to work the next day."

"Oh, that's good. Glad to hear it."

Ryan signed the last page and handed the papers back to Larry, who scrutinized them carefully. Larry placed his authorized signature at the bottom of the last page.

"Okay, you're all set. I'll fax the paperwork over to the corporate office today. The only thing to remember is you have to pay taxes and penalties on the money," he told him with a grimace of concern.

"Yeah, it's not a problem. I'll take care of it at the end of the year when I file my income tax." He shook hands with Larry and offered his goodbyes. He walked out of the office and back to his car with a proud smile. He drove home to tell Amy the good news.

Amy was angry and did not share his enthusiasm, though she knew the money could alleviate most of their financial obligations.

"Let's celebrate and get a package," he said as he walked in the living room. Amy needed a drink to calm her nerves. She grabbed two wine glasses and a bottle of cheap Zinfandel and followed him to the living room. She sat next to him on the couch. There always seemed to be a reason to celebrate good or bad news. After all, the drug addiction had become a means to an end.

He looked at her once again. "The stuff we got from Junior and Nokie really sucks. I want to try my friend Willy this time." He could sense her eyes glaring at him as he turned to the phone. He ignored her and dialed the number. He was in remarkably high spirits. He made a pipe and waited comfortably on the couch for Willy.

Amy poured two glasses of white Zinfandel, handed one to Ryan, and took a sip from her glass. "We do not have any cash. How do you plan to pay him?" she asked as she rose from the couch and switched the stereo on to listen to her favorite rock station, 100.7 WZLX.

"I thought we could sell him the TV in the bedroom. We never use it, and we can always buy another one when I get my annuity check," he told her as he went to the kitchen window, anticipating Willy's arrival. He glanced out the Venetian blinds a couple of times and returned to the couch.

"How long will it take you to get the money?" she asked.

"Larry told me I should have a check by Friday," he smiled.

How much will you give me to pay the bills?"

"We'll see. I think I can give you half," he told her, avoiding her eyes.

Amy sighed in disapproval. "Ryan I do not want to sell the TV. I watch it more than you do. When you watch sports in here, I can watch my movies in the bedroom. It's not fair to me."

"Shut up! Relax, it's just a few days," he said, truly believing it was the truth.

"Fuck off and die!" she hollered back.

"What the fuck is your problem?"

"How dare you tell me to shut up? Who the hell do you think you are?"

"Well, do you want to get high or not?"

"Yes I do, but you don't have to talk to me that way."

"What are you, a stupid fuck, or what? We can't get high without money. It's obvious we have to get money somehow, and right now that's the only way!"

"Fuck you! *You're* the stupid fuck, not me. I have a college degree. What do you have?"

"I may not have an education, but I have more friends than you do! How many friends would lend you money?"

"Good for you, you asshole!" Her tears began to flow. "Why don't you get out and go live with one of those great friends of yours?"

"Fuck you! I'm not going anywhere! *You* get out!" He laughed at her.

"Screw you! Get the fuck out! I want a divorce!" She hurled the remote control at his head. He ducked, and the remote hit the wall.

"Hey, you can leave any fucking time you want. Just don't let the door hit you in the ass on the way out." He laughed at her once more. He knew how much she hated it when he laughed at her. It drove her crazy, and he knew he could get away with it because she had no place to go. All of her family lived too far away, and she had no close friends she could trust. He wasn't foolish, though. He knew there was no place for him either. Besides, he loved her and would never leave her.

Her watery eyes, now a hazel shade, began to leak down her round cheeks, and she made a dash for the bedroom. She slammed the door hard behind her and fell on the bed, crying her eyes out. Ryan sat at the desk and played online cribbage. "Hey, if she thinks she can do better, then let her try," he mumbled under his breath.

Willy showed up within an hour. Ryan opened the door in his usual guarded manner, and Willy waltzed into the kitchen like a dancing bird of paradise. He wore denim jeans and a Black Dog sweatshirt. "So, what's up? It's been a long time," he said, hugging Ryan with a rugged embrace.

"Good, man. I got married, and I'd like to introduce you to her." Ryan called out, "Amy, please come here! I want you to meet Willy!" he said, as though nothing had happened.

She opened the bedroom door and clutched her glass of wine from the coffee table with an indifferent grin. She had no interest in meeting another drug-dealer. She watched Willy as he sat down at the kitchen table. She took a seat across from him, observing everything about his appearance. He turned quickly and gave her a friendly wink.

"Hi, I'm Willy," he said as he gave her a warm, light handshake.

He was short and heavyset with deep-set blue

eyes, black hair with a diminished hairline, and a cleft in his chin like Kirk Douglas. He wore three jeweled rings on his left hand, none of which was a wedding ring. She wondered why the drug-dealers she met all seemed to be single. It struck her like a hammer on a nail. Living in the fast lane did not afford the luxury of a normal family life, and most of them lived with the curse of having to look over their shoulder. They traveled light and quickly moved from place to place. Willy had a loud, hearty laugh, and she imagined how fun it might be to hang out with him if he was not a drug-dealer. She picked up her wine glass, sipped it slowly, and smiled at him. She liked him instantly.

"Hello, it is nice to meet you." She shook his hand and gave him a spirited smile. She offered him a glass of wine, but he politely refused. He turned and looked at Ryan.

"So what do you need?"

"I need three, but I don't have any cash right now. Will you take the flat-screen TV in the bedroom for three?" he asked, knowing Willy would say yes. The one decisive characteristic Ryan knew about Willy was that he loved a deal. Willy would sell the TV for more than what the packages were worth.

He backed up away from Ryan. "Oh, man, I don't know. I can really use the cash," he said, seeming hesitant but already knowing it was a done deal. Willy bought and sold drugs, and there was always money to make, and everyone loved a good deal. "I have to up my supply, and its cash only," he said with an artful smile.

"Come on, Willy, It's practically brand new. I bought it last fall, and it's worth more than the three packages. And you know it is, so don't break my balls."

"All right, I'll take it," Willy agreed as he slipped his hand in his right pocket and removed a Baggie containing ten mini Ziploc bags of white powder. He opened the Baggie and took out three bags. He tossed them on the table. "Here you go, and now let me see the TV."

Ryan and Willy sprang from the table and headed to the bedroom while Amy poured another glass of wine. When they reached the TV set, Ryan shouted to Amy, "How do I unhook the fucking TV from the video cassette recorder and the cable box?" He managed his business and personal affairs with a polished charm and a dazzling expertise, but when it came to electronics he was as awkward as a penguin and doltish as a turkey.

"Wait a minute! I'll be right there!" she explained loudly as she rose from the kitchen table. Uneasy as she was with helping them, she could not embarrass Ryan in front of his friend. She approached the TV and pulled the cable box slightly off the single bureau. She stretched behind the bureau and unplugged the set from the wall outlet. She reached behind the box, and after a few twists and turns it detached from the cables. All the while taking in a deep breath, she huffed and puffed with loathing at selling it to get high. She abruptly left the room.

"Thanks, baby," Ryan joked while she stomped out, not laughing at his attempt at humor. He hoisted the TV set off the bureau and handed it to Willy, who seized it under his arm. Together they walked out of the bedroom, laughing. As they strolled by Amy, she sighed in exasperation, lowered her head, and ignored their glances. Ryan smiled sarcastically and followed Willy into the kitchen. "Thanks, man," he said.

"Later, man. Call me soon. I might have some percs to sell. I'll call you."

After Willy had left with the TV, Ryan cooked two packages. This time the product came back excellent, and it took three hours to finish.

The next several days passed slowly with no money and no crack, but when Friday rolled around Ryan retrieved the mail from the box and, in the midst of bills, he found his annuity check. During the afternoon, Amy stopped at the bank, did a little grocery shopping, and caught up with the bills, including enough to turn the cable back on. When she finished the errands, she picked Ryan up for an exquisite waterfront lunch at the Venezia restaurant in Dorchester. They split an over-sized Italian antipasto with garlic bread over candlelight and finished the main course of chicken cacciatore, followed by six packages of the devil's dessert. It was a day filled with romance and harmony. It had been a year since they had enjoyed such bliss. The day ended with packages from Willy, and as the setting sun cleared the horizon, the devil seduced them once again.

The fifteen thousand lasted three short months. Half of the money went toward the bills. They paid the utilities in full, mailed the landlord an eight-hundred-dollar rent check, and bought a flat-screen TV at Best Buy. They paid off some of their debt to family and friends, and the rest went to crack. They dished out close to eight hundred dollars a week on it.

The United States economy was stagnant at best. Ryan had been out of work and dormant for four months before he finally decided to examine other employment options. He painted homes for friends and family over the years, mostly as favors. He had recently finished painting the Bennett's kitchen. He had a knack for painting, and it seemed to be his best alternative.

He checked with some friends who owned their own construction companies, but no one had any jobs. He made a stop at every hardware store in the area to see if anyone needed painters. After his third day of inquiries, he found a successful prospect on his last stop before heading home. The manager at Acme Hardware presented him with a business card for a local interior decorator. When he got home, he dialed the contractor and secured a painting position. It only paid a hundred dollars cash a day, but it helped Amy to pay the bills, and it made him feel good to know he had a job. He made plans to start the following Monday.

Ryan and Amy spent all weekend getting high before returning to work the following Monday. He left around six in the morning, wearing his white painter's pants and shirt. Amy noticed how sexy and handsome he looked in a rugged sort of way, but said nothing. She was just happy to have him working again. She spent the morning cleaning the house, and took a nap after lunch. She woke around five in the evening, just in time to have dinner with Ryan. She left at ten o'clock and drove to the hotel to start her night shift.

Ryan found it satisfying to deal with Willy again. He knew him for years, but when he became a heroin junkie and a crackhead their routine changed. They had lost touch with each other six months before Ryan married Amy, because Willy was in a halfway house. Ryan remembered some of the crazy shit they use to do together. Willy loved having Ryan drive him around while he dropped off packages to his customers.

Ryan recalled a night they drove to Revere to drop off a few packages. He drove down Revere Beach Parkway in his Chevy Camaro Z28, just shooting the shit with Willy until he dropped off the packages at a crackhouse while Ryan waited for him in the car. On the drive home to Quincy, Willy said, "Man, this is cool. I know I never met your father before he passed away, but it's awesome knowing you have your father's reputation as an FBI agent behind you." Willy laughed solidly. "I mean it, if we ever get in trouble, we'd be out of it in no time." He looked at Ryan and laughed again.

"Yeah, it does have its benefits, doesn't it? And I hope I never have to use it," Ryan said with a solemn smile as he fondly remembered his father, undoubtedly rolling over in his grave, knowing what his son turned out to be. He wished Amy had a chance to meet him before he died.

"Being with you is like having your own private insurance agent," Willy remarked with a chuckle, and turned the radio up as loud as it would go.

Ryan drove erratically and sped up like a NASCAR driver. Willy clicked in his seatbelt and pushed hard into the passenger seat as his smile faded to a grimace.

On a similar night, Willy and Ryan drove to a Dunkin' Donuts in Chelsea to score an ounce of coke. Willy spent a half an hour with his customer while Ryan waited in the car. When Willy returned, Ryan peeled out of his parking space in anger.

"Hey, Ryan, I don't mind the way you drive, but do you think you could slow the fuck down?" Willy pleaded, looking frightened.

Ryan laughed. "Chill out. It will be fine."

"You fucking nut! Slow down! I have an ounce of coke on me!" We can't afford to get pulled over by the cops."

Ryan slowed down. They were more than halfway back to Quincy when he realized he had not turned on his headlights, but for some reason the cops never pulled them over. They made it home safe, and he appreciated that they were lucky bastards.

Ryan's acquaintance with other drug-dealers was the direct result of losing touch with Willy. Several times over the years, Willy had spent weeks in detox centers trying to get clean from heroin, and quite a few months in jail for violating his probation. Now he spent three to four afternoons a week at Ryan's apartment. He cut and packaged an ounce of cocaine into mini Ziploc bags. When he finished, Ryan drove him to his prospective customers, and there were times when Ryan allowed Willy to borrow the car. This ensured freebies for Ryan and Amy, which only intensified their cravings. Free crack results in stronger addiction, and eventually more business, so Willy never minded giving them more cocaine.

On a misty night in early April, as Willy prepared his packages at the kitchen table, Ryan cooked the free gram Willy had given him. Amy nursed a glass of red wine as she sat and watched them. She hated to have Willy prepare his packages in her apartment, but she loved the free crack highs. However, she feared the police would bust in at any time and arrest them all. They were taking chances they had no business taking. Too much was at stake. She hated Willy for allowing Ryan to drive him to his customers, and she resented Ryan for letting Willy borrow the car.

Ryan finished cooking the gram of coke and looked at Willy. "You know, asshole, you need to get off the heroin. It will kill you some day. Besides, you need to think about your son and grandchildren." Ryan knew heroin was a physical addiction, while the crack was a psychological one, and most heroin junkies don't make it back, but he believed there was hope for everyone.

Willy weighed his gram and turned to Ryan. "What the fuck are you talking about? Who the fuck do you think you are? What about you? I'll quit when you do. What do you think about that?" he said, trying not to sound angry, though he was. His comments hit Ryan like a boxer's southpaw, and Ryan knew he could not quit any more than Willy could. So he shut his mouth and minded his own business.

A few days later, Amy mentioned her fears to Ryan. "I don't like Willy doing his business out of the apartment. Can we stop this shit now before it gets us in trouble?"

"Yeah, you're right. I agree it's too risky," he said, looking out the window in deep thought. "There's one problem."

"And what might that be?"

"He won't give us any more freebies," he said, looking at her like a little puppy dog.

"I don't care. Maybe we need to think about getting off the shit."

Ryan gave Willy the bad news, and the visits to the apartment stopped, along with the free cocaine. From that point on, Willy charged them for their crack. The times when money was a little short, Ryan sold his golf clubs to Willy, along with a videocassette recorder. They were right back where they had started.

Having Willy as a friend meant spending time together, and he always had a place to crash if he needed it, but he introduced Ryan and Amy to many of his girlfriends. Though most of the girls were down to earth, they all came from drug backgrounds. One in particular was a prostitute, but Amy, not a judgmental person, grew fond of her.

By the end of summer, Quincy detectives arrested Willy for violating his probation, and he spent the next year in jail. He called Ryan from prison and asked him to keep an eye on his girlfriend, but Ryan knew that while daddies are away, little girls will play. She was a party-hardy type with numerous friends, and without Willy watching over her, she died of an overdose at the age of twenty-six.

Meanwhile, Ryan and Amy chased the dragon. They smoked crack every day, stopped paying the bills, and sold everything of value. The most devastating sale came close to ruining their marriage. With every hit they took, they thought they lived in heaven, but in reality they lived on the shirttails of the devil. Amy made impromptu decisions while she was high, regretting each one after the comedown.

Late Saturday night when they finished smoking the crack they had, they began to jones. Ryan made a deal after they depleted the money. "I can sell my wedding band to Nokie," he told her with an imprudent look. "It's solid fourteen-carat gold, and he'll give me a good price of it."

"Oh, no, Ryan, please don't do that," she begged. She knew how capable he was at finding money, and it disgusted her that he could even think of selling his wedding ring.

"You want to get high, don't you?" he asked. "Let's face it—because of my work, I don't wear it anyway."

She gaped at him sheepishly, "Yes, but your

wedding ring! Don't you think that's extreme?" she asked.

"It's all we have left of value," Ryan told her. "What difference does it make now? Who knows, he might not take it. It'll get him here, and we can deal with him then."

She glanced down at the floor in deep thought. She lifted her head and stared into his eyes. "Okay, call him," she told him, knowing it was a mistake but she could not change his mind.

Ryan sold his wedding ring to Nokie for four packages—not nearly what it was worth. The devil struck again. She wanted to leave him for good that day, but the devil kept her in his trap. She knew her addiction was a fucked-up disease, because she still wanted another hit as much as he did.

By the spring of 2010, the course of their addiction began to take its toll. Ryan and Amy began to experience sharp pains in their chest that ran down their left arms, but when they smoked their next hits the pains went away. Their bodies said no, but their minds lied to them, telling them they had to have another hit, and they convinced themselves death would not come knocking at their door.

On a tepid Saturday in early May, as the flowers in the garden began to bloom and the grass turned a vibrant green, Amy decided to hold a yard sale to help pay the bills. She bought four sturdy poster boards and cut them in the shape of arrows. Inside the arrows she wrote "YARD SALE" in large black letters and nailed them to four tree trunks surrounding the neighborhood. She made a great salesperson and earned five hundred dollars from the junk in the cellar. One person's trash is always another's antique.

At the end of the day, as she closed up shop, Ryan counted the cash. "Hey, we have enough to pay the bills and get a package," he said with a smile.

"Don't even think about it," she said firmly. "I need all of it to pay the bills. The five hundred won't come close to paying what we owe."

"Come on, Amy. I'll just take two hundred," he said as he slipped the cash into to his pocket. "Just pay half the bills this month, and we'll catch up later."

As he looked at her, she was still frowning at him. Abruptly she grabbed the strong box, stormed into the apartment, and safely hid the strong box of cash under the towels in the linen closet. Not currently under the influence of a crack high, she found it painless to say no. She stayed strong, and after she had finished the night's crack, she drank three cocktails to calm her jitters. She fell asleep on the couch, which had become a routine.

Early the next morning after Ryan left for work, Amy drove to the bank, purchased money orders to pay bills, and promptly dropped them into the mailbox outside the bank.

Two weeks later, when Amy picked up her paycheck, it was three hundred dollars short. She checked all the deductions carefully and noticed a three-dollar deduction listed as 'other.' She immediately telephoned the payroll department. They informed her that the Massachusetts

Department of Revenue made a mandatory deduction for unpaid taxes. Her chin dropped to her feet. She could not believe they attached her paycheck, and it was too late to do anything to correct the problem. The state department deducted the same amount for the next six months. It slowed them down, and the crack nights dwindled.

When she returned home that afternoon, she screamed at Ryan. "What the fuck are we supposed to do now?"

As usual, Ryan apologized. "Don't worry, baby, I'll help with the bills. I promise. We won't do any more packages." She ignored him, ran out the door, and drove for hours in no apparent direction, leaving Ryan alone to dissect his life and their relationship. The packages stopped, not because they wanted them to, but because there was no money. Now they smoked crack only when Lou bought it for them.

Later in the evening, when she returned from her drive, Amy became concerned about the Internal Revenue Service. They owed them twenty-five thousand dollars. "Ryan, we must do something about the IRS," she explained to him in a condescending tone. "If the state attached my pay, it won't be long before the IRS does the same."

"I know. We'll have to call a lawyer and get it straightened out."

If the taxes were not enough of a problem, their situation continued to deteriorate.

Two weeks later, Amy went through the daily routine of morning coffee, collected the dirty clothes for the Laundromat, and grabbed her grocery list from the refrigerator door. As she opened the apartment door, she could not see her car. She walked up and down the street to see if Ryan had parked it in a different location, but she could not find it.

Ryan did not have a painting job that day and was still fast asleep in bed. Amy ran back into the apartment and frantically tried to shake him awake. "Ryan! Ryan!" she called. The few minutes it took to wake him seemed like hours to her.

"What the fuck? What's the matter?" he hollered.

"Someone stole my car!" she shouted, fear welling up in her face.

He stumbled out of bed and made his way to the door. He looked out the window and then turned to Amy. "I'll call the police." After a short conversation on the telephone, the police told him the bank had repossessed it.

He looked at Amy and shook his head in disgust. "The bank took the car. I'll drive you to work tonight and figure out what we can do for tomorrow," he said despairingly. He now realized the hole they had dug for themselves and knew it was time to try to fix it, but he had no idea how to get back on track.

In the following days, Amy drove to work with a coworker until they found a more permanent solution. With no money left in Ryan's retirement fund, she withdrew five thousand from her own and bought a decent used car, which only increased their income-tax debt.

After a year, she failed to pay the automobile

registration and insurance. She drove the car for another year without suitable coverage and feared every day the police would stop her, but somehow they never did.

Ryan and Amy smoked crack for the first fifteen years of their marriage, sold their souls to the devil, and lost everything of value except their love for one another…

Heather McCarthy

THE BEGINNING

Amy stood at her father's grave, eyeing the bouquet of roses on the casket, scrutinizing her last fifteen years of marriage to Ryan. As much as she loved her father and sensed an uncontrollable loss, he was but an angel in a mask. His health had failed rapidly over the past year, and because her brother cared for him, he had willed all of his money to her brother. Though she never understood the reason, she never saw one copper penny of it. She could not imagine the depth of her father's cruelty, but accepted his betrayal because she had no other recourse. She had no money to hire a lawyer and dispute the will, so she learned to live without the money. Her brother flew back to Florida three days after the funeral without discussing the will. He conveniently disappeared from her life, and she never saw or spoke to him again. If she had acquired an inheritance, she knew they were sure to blow it on the devil.

Amy eventually hired a lawyer, but it took two years and money she did not have to obtain a copy of her father's will. She had to borrow money from the Bennetts to pay off the lawyer. She hoped her half of the inheritance would alleviate the financial burden of the IRS and the car, but it was a disappointment.

She decided to put it all behind her. She could

not regain the lost years and finally realized that the power to control the future lay somewhere deep within her soul. She had to find a way to climb out of the tumultuous hole they had dug.

The weekend after the funeral, Ryan's sister Patti invited them for dinner. Ryan and Amy made their way to Patti's modern-style split-level ranch and found the front door ajar. They knocked once, softly pushed the door open, and yelled, "Hello!"

"Hi there, come on in!" Patti yelled back from the top of the small flight of stairs. Ryan went up and met Patti and her husband as Amy followed, and they all tightly hugged each other. Ryan and Amy wandered past the colonial kitchen into the cozy living room as Patti offered them a drink. Ryan took a Coors Light, and Amy settled for a glass of water. Ryan and Patti's mother, who occupied an in-law apartment adjacent to Patti's home, joined them for dinner. She entered, embracing Ryan and Amy.

The serene atmosphere reminded Ryan of his childhood. By the time he was in the second grade, he had marched by his father's side in the annual Memorial Day parade in honor of his brothers, who at the time were Marines fighting in Vietnam. When he was fourteen, he played the ponies with his father at the Suffolk Downs racetrack, and his principal suspended him from school for carrying a racing form in his back pocket. At sixteen, Ryan was an average shooter at the Braintree Rifle and Pistol Club, and his father bought him his first weapon. He missed his father and visited his mother often just to shoot the shit.

They all sat on the oversized couch and made light chitchat as they waited for Patti to serve dinner. She prepared a roast beef, hot rolls with melted butter, mashed potatoes, and butternut squash with a touch of cinnamon. It was a meal fit for an emperor. It had been a long time since the family enjoyed a home-cooked meal together, unlike some he shared with Amy—they ate at fast-food restaurants most of the time, and when she cooked meals at home, they hardly ate before smoking crack. Breakfast was usually the previous night's leftovers.

After enjoying the main course, Amy helped Ryan's mother clear the table while Patti remained seated, gazing at Ryan. "So, Ryan what's up with you lately?" she asked him frankly, concerned with his rebuff of many of her invitations. His mother stood at the kitchen sink, turned her head, and looked intently at her son's face. She waited patiently to hear what he had to say.

"What do you mean?" he asked, knowing full well what she meant.

"Come on, Ryan. Tell me what's going on," Patti prodded, mystified with her brother's denial.

Before long, Ryan dropped a sandbag and told them about his addiction. "I have been a crack addict for thirty years," he confessed. "I started snorting coke in high school, and one weekend, in my senior year, some friends turned me on to smoking the shit. It's like nothing I ever tried before, and the devil grabbed me by the balls. It's not something I'm proud of, but it is the truth. I have done some terrible things over the years. I have been an asshole, and

God bless Amy for putting up with me for all these years," he concluded as a tear began to flow from his eye. He bowed his head in shame for destroying his family's trust in him.

Everyone at the table began to cry. "I knew there was something wrong," Patti whimpered and coughed across the table. "We didn't want you to think you were fooling anyone. We knew the shit you were up to, all the missed family parties and the excuses."

His mother shook her head. "So do you have any plans to stop this shit?" she prodded. "Have you tried to get any help?"

"Not yet, mum, but I'm working on it," he said.

"You're my son, and I'll never stop loving you. I can only pray that you find your way, and soon," she articulated, hoping he would heed her words. She could not bear to lose him over something so stupid. She had loved and pampered her son for most of his life. Now she felt regret to think she was the cause of his troubles, but down deep she knew he had to find his own way.

Amy remained silent and demure. His family took in everything he had said, and the mood in the room changed to a solemn semblance. They all devoured the hot apple pie Ryan's mother had baked and moved to the living room, where Ryan changed the subject and spent another hour discussing various topics of personal interest over a few more beers.

After giving everyone a hug at the end, Ryan and Amy left for the apartment.

They managed to remain crack free for the next

week. She truly believed that if they could stop for a week, then why not longer? Yet she understood what every drug addict knows. When you're broke, it is always easy to stay clean. Amy wanted to stop, and now that Ryan's family knew about his addiction, she thought they might have a chance. She hated living this way and knew if Ryan could just stop buying the shit, she would have no problem quitting. She was more than ready now.

Ryan visited his mother every week, and on the next Sunday afternoon when he pulled up in front of Patti's house, he noticed several parked cars in the driveway and along the street. He got out of his car and knocked on Patti's door. For a long time, no one answered. Confused and irritated, he started down the front steps when Patti opened the door.

Surprise and guilt shadowed Patti's face, and she blushed. "Oh, Ryan, hello. I wasn't expecting you."

"That seems pretty obvious," he said, indiscreetly straining his neck to peer into the house for a closer look. "Are you having friends over?" He felt embarrassed that he had intruded on her, but he started to hear voices he recognized.

"Well, no," she hesitated. "It's not friends. We are having a small family get together," she said carefully. "I would invite you in, but I don't think that's a good idea right now."

"What's up? What's going on?" he probed, frowning while looking her squarely in the face.

"To be completely honest with you, I cannot have anyone in my house or near my grandchildren that does drugs." She began to cry and shake her head uneasily. "I'm truly sorry, Ryan, but I just can't do it. Get yourself straightened out first. Once you do that, we will talk."

"Don't apologize," he smiled contritely. "I guess I can't blame you, and I'm sorry I caused you to feel that way."

"Goodbye, Ryan." She choked on the words as the tears trickled down her cheeks. She turned around and slowly closed the door. She hated to reject him so coldly, but had no choice. She was a forgiving woman by nature, but had her family to think about, and Ryan stepped over the line.

Depressed, Ryan drove home and plunged himself deeper into the crack. The painting jobs dried up, and he started to smoke every day. He slipped into Amy's pocketbook and lifted her ATM card to withdraw money. Amy tried to work with him to stop, and as difficult as it was for her, at times she refused to get high with him. She did the best she could, but it always seemed hopeless. The devil kept drawing her back. It did not last long. She found it tough to stop when he was bringing the shit into the house.

When he exhausted her bank account, he managed to find another alternative.

Lou picked up his paycheck and cashed it every Thursday before starting his late afternoon shift. During his dinner break, he called Ryan ahead of time to place a package order and, with perfect regularity, showed up at the apartment after work to party. After a few weeks, Ryan intentionally concocted a change in Junior's schedule. He no longer delivered after six in the evening. Ryan could now make the trip into downtown Boston and pick up Lou's cash.

The city, with its numerous one-way streets, had little-to-no parking, and Ryan double-parked on Boylston Street until he saw Lou emerge from the Prudential Center. Lou stepped into the passenger side of the car, and Ryan drove cautiously around the block while Lou handed him his money. Countless drug deals went down this way, and Ryan was no amateur. Unfortunately, after Ryan returned home, he bought the packages with Lou's money and smoked half of it with Amy before Lou arrived at the apartment. On the nights she needed to work, she either called in sick or arrived at work high as the clouds. The new routine lasted for several weeks, and eventually Lou stopped calling. Between the crack coming back like shit and Ryan smoking half of it, Lou realized he was paying for more product than he was smoking.

At the suggestions of friends, Ryan and Amy tried several attempts to attend both Narcotics and Alcoholics Anonymous. They listened to other addicts tell their all-too-familiar stories. After the meetings and before they left the parking lot, Ryan was on the phone trying to call dealers for a package. Knowing that sitting in a meeting was the right thing to do, he was still not interested in doing the right thing.

This vicious circle persisted with lie after lie, telling friends and family what they wanted to hear just to get them off his back. Almost at every meeting, more than one speaker said, "You can only stop when you're ready, no one can force you or tell you when and where." It was a hard lesson to learn, and Ryan knew many who never made it back.

It was early Wednesday evening when Amy heard Ryan cough uncontrollably. She ran from the bedroom and found him choking.

"Ryan, what's wrong?" she cried out.

He struggled to speak. "I—can't—breathe," he said slowly and gaspingly.

"Stand up and see if you can breathe," she said, standing by his side and, with some difficulty, helping him to his feet. He stopped coughing, but his breathing was still shallow. He started to breathe heavily again, gasping for air.

Amy picked up the telephone and dialed 911. The ambulance arrived ten minutes later. The paramedics placed Ryan on oxygen and rushed him to the hospital with Amy in close pursuit. The Emergency Triage unit responded immediately. The nurses wheeled him on a stretcher to a cubicle and prepped him with intravenous fluids and heart monitors. Amy paced nervously back and forth in the waiting room, anxious to hear if he was dead or alive.

Thirty minutes later, the Triage nurse emerged from the large sliding doors and approached Amy. "Mrs. O'Connor, your husband is in stable condition. We are monitoring his heart and breathing." Amy gave her a relieved smile.

"Can I see him?" she asked with a hopeful plea on her pale face. She lacked trust in the nurse's words and needed reassurance.

"Yes, I think it will be fine. He's waiting for the doctor to finish reading his chart. Go through the double doors, and he's in the second bed on your right."

"Thank you." Amy smiled nervously at the nurse and hurried through the double sliding doors. The patient in the first room had the curtain draped, and as she reached the second, she found Ryan sitting up with an oxygen tube in his nose and electrodes on his chest. She did not have a strong stomach and hated to see people or animals suffer, which is why she had not entered the field of medicine. She had enough brains for it but grimaced at the sight of blood.

She rushed to his side, placed his cheeks between her palms, and kissed him hard on his clammy forehead. Her whole body trembled as she stepped away from him and asked, "Are you okay?"

"Yeah, I'm good now," he told her as a smile of reassurance came over his face.

"Did they say what was wrong with you?"

"No, I'm waiting for the doctor."

"I was so worried about you. I thought I lost you," she said softly, a hint of relief he might be out of danger.

His smile faded the moment she turned her back. He tried to hide his anxiety from her. He had finally come face-to-face with his own mortality.

In the next moment, a dynamic and lean man entered his room. "Hello, I'm Doctor Goldstein," he said, looking at Ryan and exchanging a handshake with him. Twice he turned and quickly glanced at

Amy, but never addressed her directly. He looked at Ryan's medical chart once more, and then turned to Amy. "Mrs. O'Connor, could you please step outside for a second while I speak to your husband." She threw him a discontented stare and looked back at Ryan.

Ryan rolled his eyes and gave her a "do not worry" look that she understood. He turned to face the doctor. "My wife doesn't have to leave. I have no secrets from her."

"I understand, but I would still like her to step outside. Just for a moment," the doctor told Ryan firmly.

Amy sulked, shrugged her shoulders, and left the room without another word. She quietly stood on the other side of the curtain and listened intently to their conversation. The doctor spoke softly, but Amy heard every word.

The doctor handed Ryan a pen and notepad. "Okay, Mr. O'Connor, please write down what has been going on. Why are you here?" As the doctor began his examination, Ryan plainly wrote: *Thirty years' cocaine abuse.* The doctor placed the stethoscope on Ryan's chest and listened to his heart. He quickly checked his neck, pulse, and legs. Ryan handed the notepad back to the doctor, who glanced at Ryan's scribble. He paused, removed his eyeglasses, and stared at his patient with a skeptical look. As he pointed to the number thirty, he looked straight into Ryan's eyes. "Is this number right?" he asked in disbelief. The doctor shook his head in amazement. He had never met a patient who had survived thirty years of drug abuse.

Ryan gazed at him with a tear in his eye and said, "Yes. I'm afraid it is. I smoked crack for thirty years."

The doctor nodded his head. "Well Mr. O'Connor, it appears you may have damaged your heart. I would like to admit you to the hospital for a few days and perform extensive tests to discover the amount of the damage."

"All right," Ryan said, drawing a deep breath. As the doctor left the room to process Ryan's admission to the hospital, he passed by Amy, not saying a word. Amy returned to Ryan's bedside. Ryan looked at her with wide-open eyes. "He wants to admit me."

"I heard. I'm sure it is the best thing for you right now. He does not seem to be especially friendly."

"What do you expect? He can't believe I smoked crack for thirty years and lived to tell about it." She knew the time had come to change their lifestyle. She sat in the chair next to the bed and held his hand. It had crossed her mind many times to stop smoking crack, but she needed something to happen that could force Ryan into her way of thinking. The outcome could be good, and she hoped she would not lose Ryan in the process. It would not be an easy transition, but she still loved him, and their marriage was worth saving. Now she really thought it was time to dig their way out.

They wheeled Ryan to his room, and he remained in the hospital for five days. Amy never left his side. He suffered from minor withdrawal symptoms for the first two days. By the third day, he had a new roommate— which, unfortunately, happened to be a drug-dealer. He offered his telephone number and a good deal on packages. Ryan took the number and placed it in his overnight bag.

On the third morning, the doctor diagnosed Ryan with congestive heart failure and minimal heart damage. He gave him seven prescriptions to monitor his blood pressure and his heart, and he maintained a monthly schedule of blood tests. Ryan left the hospital in good spirits, and they stopped at a local pancake house for breakfast. When they reached home, he slipped into bed for a nap. Amy unpacked his overnight bag and found a telephone number.

"Ryan, where did you get this telephone number?" she asked him.

"It's nothing. Just throw it out. I don't need it anymore," he told her. Amy left and closed the door to the bedroom. She threw the paper into the kitchen wastebasket and made a cup of herbal tea.

Ryan stayed clean for a week. On the weekend after they released him from the hospital, he dialed Nokie.

"What the fuck are you doing?" she screamed. "Are you out of your fucking mind? You almost died, you asshole!"

"Don't start with me!" he told her. "I feel fine! One little package won't hurt us!"

"You're fucking crazy! I don't want any, so count me out!" She was not about to be bullied by him any longer. She wanted out, and she dug deep within herself to find the courage to say no. It was not easy for her, but she managed to step back and take hold of her own life. "He's going to die, and there is nothing I can do to stop it," she whispered under her breath. She felt helpless, but she was all done, even if he was not.

Just as soon as he finished his first hit, he realized what an asshole he had been, but it did not stop him from finishing the package. Amy sat on the couch, watching TV, a tear in her eye. There was nothing left for her to do except stop, and she gave up trying to convert him. Ryan went to bed, and Amy fell asleep on the couch, as usual.

Ryan awoke the next morning feeling worse than ever. Realizing how hard it was to let go of an addiction, he picked up the coke plate and the homemade pipe. He walked to the kitchen and threw everything in the wastebasket. He made the coffee and started breakfast.

Amy rose slowly from the couch as the aroma of hot coffee filled her nostrils. She walked through the kitchen to the bathroom without saying a word to her husband. She showered, dressed, and took a seat at the kitchen table. Ryan passed her a cup of coffee and a plate of bacon, eggs and toast. He took a seat beside her and put his hand over hers.

"I think it's safe to say I'm done," he said.

"Do we have to talk about this now?" she said, pushing his hand away. "You'll never stop. You almost died, and you still bought another package."

"Yes. We need to talk. I promise I'll never buy another package."

"I need to brush my hair and put on my makeup,"

she said, angry and flustered. She started to stand, and Ryan grabbed her hand, pulling her back into her chair.

"Look at me," he told her with a warm glow on his face. She refused to look at him. "I mean it, Amy, look at me." She turned and glanced at his face. "Look me in the eyes," he said. She did. "I promise I'll never buy another package. I don't want to lose you. I do mean it this time. I love you."

Amy smiled warmly. It had been a long time since she had heard him profess his love for her. "You promise?" she asked, looking directly into his eyes.

Yes. It is the beginning of a new life for us, and I promise it will be better. Do you still love me?" he asked nervously, praying she would give him the answer he needed and wanted to hear. He loved her more than life itself, but over the years he had owned their situation, and he placed her in a near-impossible relationship. He did not think he could bear it if she said no.

"My love might change like the direction of a tornado or even a fisherman's lure, but I'll never stop loving you."

Amy thought it was a miracle that Ryan stopped smoking crack and tried to send the devil back to hell. She did not understand how he did it, but like magic, without one day of rehabilitation or counseling, he went cold turkey. Ryan understood. He recognized that his mortality proved to be a powerful motivator, and it seemed to bring about a life change in him. They had struggled each day with crack urges and seemed to conquer one demon, but they still had a long road to full recovery. He had always been close to his family, and when his sister rejected him, he realized what he lost.

To stay on their chosen path, they attended weekly meetings at a local place called Life House. They attended together for a month until Amy decided she did not need them anymore. Ryan continued for another month.

After one of his meetings, he stopped to pick up appetizers at a local Chinese restaurant. While having a beer, he heard karaoke singing in the back of the bar. Being a Tuesday night, there were only two customers in the lounge. Like most people, Ryan sang only in the shower. But after hearing the karaoke host sing, Ryan decided he wanted to try a tune. He stepped on a small wooden platform, held the microphone to his mouth, and belted out "I Left My Heart in San Francisco."

After a few more beers and a couple of songs, the karaoke host approached Ryan and said, "You have a great voice, but I think you would sound much better with a Frank Sinatra song. Your voice has the right pitch, the women love you, and you have a magnetic personality."

"Thank you, but I'm not that good."

"Believe me, Ryan. You're incredibly good," the host told him.

Ryan smiled, shook his hand, and took the microphone once again. He sang Sinatra's "Summer Wind." Everyone in the lounge, along with the restaurant customers in the dining room, began to clap and whistle.

THE CARIBBEAN

In the ensuing months, singing after his meetings became a ritual, and it kept him clean. Ryan bounced back and forth between two karaoke bars in Weymouth, a small suburb south of Boston. He loved being on the stage and singing to an audience. He sang the swooning love songs of Frank Sinatra, and the women fell in love with him. His parents had raised him on the great sounds of The Rat Pack, and he also enjoyed performing the tunes of Dean Martin, Tony Bennett, and Johnny Mathis. This experience boosted his self-esteem. He found a confidence he never knew he had—but some of his friends were not so lucky.

After his release from prison, Willy was on a straight-and-narrow path. He spent six months in a halfway house. Though he had disappointed his mother time after time, she agreed to let him move in with her, because he was still her son. He stopped selling cocaine, but quietly revived his heroin habit. He managed to keep it from his family and Ryan. Fresh out of rehabilitation, his prescribed medication of Suboxone for heroin treatment was just not enough. He wanted the real McCoy.

Early Thursday afternoon, Willy telephoned Ryan. "Hey buddy, how are you?"

"Good, Willy. What's up? How are you?" Ryan

inquired, worried that Willy wanted to sell him a package. After all, Ryan had known him too long not to realize he called because he needed something.

"I have some Suboxone," Willy said. "I'm broke and need some cash. Do you know anyone who could use them?"

"Willy, I really don't know anyone, and I don't want to get involved in that shit. Amy and I are clean. Do you need the money for the junk?"

"No, no, man. I just got out of a halfway house, and my mother left on a cruise two days ago. I'm broke, and I really need the cash, man," he begged.

"Okay Willy, I can come by Saturday and throw you a few bucks. We can be normal for once, have a beer, and shoot the shit," he said.

"Sounds great, man. With Mum on a cruise, I have the whole house to myself. It'll be good to see you." His voice sounded sharp and clear.

On the drive to Willy's house, Ryan looked forward to seeing his friend, because he was proud to show off his sobriety. He wanted to hug his friend and hoped it might be an incentive for Willy to be strong. Ryan walked up Willy's porch steps with a six-pack of Budweiser and banged on the front door several times, growing increasingly impatient when Willy did not answer the door. "Where the fuck is he!" he yelled at the locked door. He stepped off the porch and walked to the back door. He knocked two more times; again, no answer. "That motherfucker, I told him I'd be here. Where the fuck is he!" he shouted again to another locked door. "Goddamn it, I'm out of here," he muttered angrily under his breath as he walked back to his car.

Arriving home a few minutes later, Ryan opened a beer. He called Willy several times throughout the day, but no answer.

Early Monday morning, the phone rang. Before Ryan raised the receiver all the way to his ear, he heard crying from the other end. "Hello? Hello?" he said, as the crying persisted.

As the caller regained her composure, he realized it was Willy's daughter-in-law. "What's wrong?" he asked, knowing in his gut it was not good news.

"Ryan, I'm so sorry to tell you, but he's gone," the caller told him, crying again.

"Who's gone?"

"Willy. His son found him dead on the kitchen floor. They think he was there for two days."

"I'm so sorry," he said, his heart filling with sadness and regret. He could not decide whether to cry or shout. Hatred and sorrow flooded him simultaneously. He knew that after talking to Willy he had already started back on the junk. Willy had let everyone down.

"I can't tell you how I feel," Ryan said. "There are no words." He realized then why Willy had not answered the door. He was already dead in the house. "I have to go right now, but please let me know about the funeral arrangements."

"Is it Willy? He's dead, right?" Amy asked sorrowfully.

"Yeah, they found him on the floor in the kitchen. He OD'd."

"Oh, Ryan, I'm sorry. That is too bad," she said

softly with compassion.

"Yes. I know it wasn't his fault, but just the devil at work. He succeeded in taking another one of our friends." Ryan turned his face away and cried. "I'm so fucking glad we quit," he whispered through his sobs.

A few days later, Ryan and Amy attended Willy's funeral and showed their last respects. On the ride home, Ryan steadied his hands on the steering wheel in humble silence. He turned to Amy and offered her a pensive palm. She placed her hand in his, and, with the right mix of eagerness and enlightenment, he spoke softly.

"You know, for all the times we got high, and took that last hit despite the chest pains, the concept of death never entered my mind. The reality of my life is painful, and I shiver when I think of the things I did. I want to focus on the future and our new goals."

Amy nodded her head in agreement and smiled at him as she squeezed his hand tightly.

Four days after the funeral, Ryan drifted by Willy's grave. As he stood there praying, he realized, how could a crackhead tell a junkie what was right or wrong? He stood in the empty cemetery and spoke softly. "The true reality is that no matter how often I hear it; there is only one person who can get the devil off your back. It's a fact that lies deep within a person's soul." He stared at the gravestone and softly whispered, "We were both out of control, buddy. I didn't make many attempts over thirty years to get help. I'm sorry our friendship ended so abruptly.

You were more than my dealer; you were also a friend. I'll miss you." He walked back to the car and thought about a new life with Amy.

A few months later, the owner of the Chinese restaurant where Ryan had made a splash at karaoke approached him. "My brother owns a restaurant in Quincy, and they have karaoke every Sunday and Thursday night. You might want to try it," he suggested.

"Really. Thanks. Maybe I'll check it out."

His love of singing and encouragement from his audience sent him in search of other outlets as well. Over the next six months, he befriended a group of fellow singers and began a new life. He sang three to four nights a week at numerous venues in Quincy, Weymouth, and Hingham. He established a completely new set of friends. Most were drug-free and some were recovering addicts. The support group at Life House talked about them, and he knew what a trigger was, but now he learned firsthand how to deal with them. He kept away from Lou and any other friends who used cocaine. Over the course of time, the dealers stopped calling, and Ryan removed any connections that tempted him.

At one particular restaurant, he met a woman who loved his voice, and each week she inspired him to sing better. His confidence and his choice of songs grew. He substituted his obsession for crack with a new addiction—love for music.

One night Ryan took the stage in a local Quincy establishment. He poured his heart and soul into to a song by Engelbert Humperdinck, "After the Lovin'."

When he returned to his seat, his new friend complimented him. "Ryan that song was so beautiful," she said with honesty and admiration. "I just entered a karaoke contest, and I've been still looking for singers. I want you to try out."

"I don't think so. I'm not that good," Ryan snickered sarcastically. Yet she was a warm, easygoing woman with her own singing ability, and if he did not do it for himself, he could do it for her. He had no choice but to agree with her. Besides, what did he have to lose?

"Oh, yes you are," she cheered. "Did you hear the clapping and whistling from the audience? They love you, and you're better than you think. Please come with me next Saturday night and try out. Please," she softly begged with a tilted head and smile. "You have nothing to lose."

"Okay, how does it work?" he asked.

"You sing in front of a panel of three judges, and each week they tally your score. If you're good enough, they ask you to come back each week. You have to exceed the previous week's score. It lasts six weeks, and you try to better your score each week. They award six prizes for the top three men and women. If you make it to the top three, they invite you to Texas for the National Championship."

"I'll go with you and cheer you on, but I'm not sure if I'll sing," he told her with the threat of reservation. "I think I'll just watch."

The following week, Ryan registered for the contest and listened to the superior voices of eight singers. His head filled with doubt, and he turned to

Amy. "What the hell am I doing here?" he said. "These people have sung their whole lives, and I suck compared to them."

"You have a wonderful voice," she said. "You have as much chance of winning as they do. It will also give you a chance to find out what true professionals think of your voice."

"I appreciate the vote of confidence, but you're wrong. I just started singing six months ago. I can't compete with these people. I saw one singer in the bathroom stretching his voice like he was an opera singer."

When the master of ceremonies called his name, he found the confidence to take the stage. The multicolored lights began to flash and swirl around his body. The music reverberated from the professional sound system, and Amy imagined she was at the Bank of America Pavilion enjoying a live concert. Ryan placed the microphone inches from his mouth and sang "After the Lovin' " to a panel of three judges, which included two women and one man. When he finished, the judges evaluated his performance.

The male judge said, "Ryan I liked your choice of song, but I think you need to slow it down. A little softer, perhaps," he added. "I'm looking forward to hearing what you have planned for next week."

The female judge commented, "Ryan, you have a strong instrument, and you would do well in the theater. You were a bit off key in the middle. Your sound is smooth, but I think you need to practice a bit more."

The second female judge said, "Mr. O'Connor, I agree with the other members of the panel, and I would just like to add that I thought your song choice could be better."

When the last judge finished his appraisal, the MC asked, "So Ryan, tell us a little bit about yourself," the MC asked.

"Well, I'm from Quincy, and I have worked as a painter for the last six months," Ryan said.

"How long have you been singing?"

"I only started singing several months ago."

"Wow, you have a great voice for only six months. Where the hell have you been?"

"Well, up until six months ago I had other priorities. I was a drug addict for thirty years, but I kicked the habit and found karaoke. Now that I'm drug-free, I sing a few nights a week."

"Great job, and I'm glad you found us. Good luck."

"Thank you," Ryan said and left the stage, disappointed. He returned to the table and sat next to Amy. "That sucked," he grumped.

"I disagree," she said adamantly, smiling with admiration. "I think you sounded good, and the first judge wants you to come back next week."

"No way!" he told her firmly. "I'm way out of my league. I'm not coming back. I never took a lesson, and I haven't sung long enough. I'll try to take some lessons and come back next year."

"Well, I think you're making a mistake, but do what you want," Amy said, dismayed that he buckled under the pressure. His confidence left him, and the thought of professionals tearing him apart made him nervous.

"I'll never go back there," Ryan said on the ride home.

"I'm sorry to hear you say that, but I think you should think about it. You have a whole week to practice and find new songs. You might have a change of heart."

"We'll see, but I doubt it."

When Amy awoke late the next morning, she prepared her coffee in the usual manner and unlocked the mailbox. She found an urgent letter from the IRS. With a weary sigh and a disgusted look she tore open the envelope.

She read slowly:

Mrs. Amy O'Connor,

> *This letter is to inform you that the Department of Internal Revenue Service will place a levy on your wages and property. If you do not contact this office within seven days to make payment arrangements, we will proceed without further notice.*

She flung the letter on the maple coffee table, sat on the couch, and sipped her coffee until Ryan woke. She knew the time had come to stop avoiding the IRS. There was no way she could afford the extra deduction from her paycheck. All she seemed to think about now was how to get a package, having found it hard to deal with reality without first getting high. Yet she shook her head and quickly brushed the thought from her mind.

When a sleepy-eyed Ryan emerged from the bedroom, she told him, "We got a demand for payment from the IRS, and they're going to attach my paycheck."

"For Pete's sake, Amy, can you let me get some coffee first before you start on me?" She frowned at his agitation and held her tongue. "Did you make coffee?" he asked.

"Yes I did," she said purely, without any feeling. The IRS was an important issue for her, and she disliked his cavalier attitude. He returned to the living room with their coffee and sat beside her.

"Now what's going on?" he asked, and leaned in to kiss her. "Whatever it is, we will deal with it."

She kissed him good morning. "The IRS is going to attach my paycheck if we don't contact them within seven days. If they take my money, I can't pay the bills," she told him fairly, and with anguish in her voice.

"How much do we own them?" he asked abruptly.

"The letter said with penalties and accrued interest, we own sixty thousand dollars. It's too much money. What are we going to do?"

Ryan placed his arms around her and drew her into his chest. "Don't worry," he soothed her. "I'll fix it. I can call my brother-in-law, and he can recommend an accountant. We'll work it out."

Having put her through so much over the years, he needed to find some way to make it up to her.

"What did we ever do to deserve each other?" he asked with a boyish grin.

"I don't know, but I wish I hadn't done it," she smiled. "He glared at her in surprise. "You do realize I'm only joking?" she said, smiling sincerely.

He smiled back at her and plainly answered, "Yes." They laughed hard and hugged each other. "I think the right thing to do now is go to church," he urged. "We can make the eleven o'clock service at St. John's. Let's get dressed and go."

Shortly after they started their Life House meetings, they began attending church every Sunday, which supported their recovery process. After the services, they always had Sunday brunch at a local eatery.

As soon as they returned to the apartment after brunch, Ryan called his brother-in-law.

On Wednesday morning they met with an accountant who suggested a tax attorney. He made a quick telephone call and scheduled an appointment for the following Tuesday. Amy telephoned the IRS as soon as she got home and, after an hour of remaining on hold, temporarily agreed to a payment plan to keep them from attaching her paycheck. She relaxed, and her panic subsided. They needed to make some serious decisions in the next few days, and she did not know if she could handle it without getting high. Life had seemed easy when she was high, when she never seemed to worry about the bills.

Two days later, however, it was time to think about Ryan's next performance. They ate an early dinner, spent a quiet evening at home with a glass of Merlot, and discussed the karaoke contest. "Now what?" she asked him.

"I don't know. It's not an experience I want to relive," he added. "What do you think I should do?"

"You have a wonderful crooning voice. You don't realize how good you really are, and all the women love you. People, mainly women, are drawn to the sound of your voice. You have both charisma and voice to give anyone a run for their money."

"Thanks for the vote of confidence, but I still don't think I'm good enough. You don't understand or know what it's like. It sucks getting up in front of thirty people who sing better than me, not to mention three judges tearing you to shreds."

"Don't exaggerate. There were only eight singers. All I ask is that you try it and see what happens. You have nothing to lose. We can go to the Last Call Lounge a couple of nights this week, and I can help you practice."

"All right. Just once more." She never felt more pleased to help. He needed her support more now than ever before. "And besides, the first prize is five hundred dollars, and we can use the money. If you win, you'll get a chance to go to Texas and compete in the National Karaoke Contest."

"My God, Amy, are you crazy?" He stared at her as though she had lost all her senses. He loved her optimism, but knew it was fruitless. "I could never win in a million years. Can you stop thinking that far ahead and let me get through at least one competition at a time?" He loved her strength, but knew how disappointed she would be when he lost.

After a light dinner on Friday night, they showered and dressed. Amy emerged from the bedroom, looking as lovely as she did when they had first met. She pulled her hair back with a comb and meticulously applied her makeup. She chose a backless sea-green dress, which complemented the swaying ginger ponytail. Ryan could not help but stare at her. "You look absolutely gorgeous," he said, noticing every curve of her slender body. "I love the dress. It makes you look ten years younger."

Though age, drug abuse and congestive heart failure had changed his good looks—he had gained another hundred pounds over the last ten months, and his hair had turned completely grey—she still found him sexy and attractive. "Thank you, dear," she said. "And don't you look good enough to eat," she teased him. He wore a black tailored shirt, slightly opened at the neck, and perfectly pressed beige trousers. She enjoyed the idea of a date. It reminded her of when they had first met.

"Yeah, Yeah. Thanks," he sneered, brushing her aside as his nerves started to gather speed. "Let's get going, or we'll be late. I have to register my song choice before someone else takes it. Do you remember from last week? No one can sing the same song."

"Yes, but don't be nervous. You'll be awesome," she reassured him as they left the apartment and headed south down Route 28 to Randolph.

The contest venue was a combination restaurant and nightclub. Upon entering it, they joined his friend who had suggested the contest. They found a seat and ordered drinks. The audience was considerably larger since the previous week, and the fight for first place had escalated. This time, thirty singers were not an exaggeration.

The lights dimmed. The spotlight shined on center stage. The music boomed. The time had come for everyone to show his or her talent.

"I would like to welcome everyone to the second annual South Shore Idol contest," the MC announced. The room exploded with clapping, whistles and loud cheers. "Everyone will get to sing one song. I want to remind each of you that you must stay on the stage until the judges have finished with their comments. They will tabulate the scores and notify you if you qualify for next week's show. Now it's time to bring our first singer to the stage."

He called a beautiful young woman who the week before had sung as beautifully as Whitney Houston. Ryan could only be thankful he was not the first singer.

When the fifth singer had finished, the MC called Ryan up. As he crossed the dance floor to the stage, Amy heard the murmurs of the crowd sweep across the room. "Who is he?" they asked in a whisper. "We've never seen him before." The rainbow of lights flashed and circled the stage. The soft melody of Frank Sinatra flowed from the speakers, and Ryan held the microphone. He belted out "Fly Me to the Moon" perfectly.

When he finished singing, the crowd began to whistle and clap. Some of the singers did not attend the previous week because their scores were so high they did not need to compete every week. Talented singers came from all over the eastern seaboard, and Amy felt proud to know Ryan was among them.

"Ryan, what a great job, but now let's see what the judges have to say," the MC announced to the crowd.

The male judge said, "Ryan I loved the song choice. You held the notes perfectly, and I look forward to seeing what you have in store for us next week. Nice job."

The female judge commented, "I think you did a better job this week than last. Every time I hear your wonderful old classic songs, I'm entertained. You have a well-tuned instrument, and I can't believe you have only been singing for six months. Good job, and I too look forward to next week."

The second female judge stated, "Ryan I thought your song was nice, but I have heard you sing two old classics, and I would really like to see you mix it up a little. I'd like to see you do something more upbeat. I think maybe next week I'd like to hear you do some Eric Clapton, or maybe some country."

"Thank you," he said honestly and returned to the table.

Ryan sat at the table, and Amy planted a hard kiss upon his dry lips. "That was awesome," she told him.

"You really think so?" he asked doubting his own ability.

"Yes, and I could tell by the judges' faces they liked it too. The last female judge didn't seem thrilled, but I know you have the other two judges in your corner. Maybe next week you could try something different."

"Yes, I suppose I can. We'll see," he said as a thoughtful gaze flushed his face.

When they returned home, Amy was tired and passed out on the couch. Ryan picked her up, slipped her dress off, and carried her to the bed. He slid her naked form under the bed sheets.

She woke the next morning smiling. She was still thinking about Ryan's performance. She knew he had potential, but he had to find it out for himself.

He competed the next week with Eric Clapton's "I've Got a Rock 'n' Roll Heart," and the judges loved him. Each week his scores improved. He held his own, and the week before the final competition, his score tabulated at 75 out of a possible 100. Many other talented singers joined the contest with the final night approaching, and he feared he would lose his standings. His hopes for a spot in the top three had been crushed.

Ryan and Amy scheduled several meetings with the tax attorney over the course of the contest. The attorney stopped the levy on Amy's pay, but it would take a year before the situation became final. Eventually they settled negotiations, and the IRS problems did go away. Ryan did not wish to make known the terms of the agreement to family and friends.

The evening before the last night of competition,

Ryan turned to Amy as they finished dinner. "I want you to listen to me carefully," he said firmly. She tried to brush him off with a nod of her shoulders. "Look at me," he said with a stern tone. "No matter what the terms are for paying back the IRS, I do not want you to tell anyone. It is our business, and no one else's. Do you understand me?" he asked her tersely. The look on his face told her she must agree.

"Fine, I understand, but what am I supposed to say when someone asks me what happened?" she inquired delicately.

"Just tell them it is over and we worked it out. That's all anybody needs to know. Look at me, and promise me you'll do as I ask?"

She looked at him sheepishly. "Okay, I promise."

As far as anyone knew, Ryan and Amy worked it out, and neither of them ever disclosed the terms of the arrangement to anyone.

The final night of competition arrived. Nervous energy filled Ryan, and he selected three shirts from his crowded closet. He threw each one on the bed with apprehension. Finally, Amy searched the closet and picked the pink dress shirt she had bought last week. "Here," she said as she lay it on the bed, "this one is perfect."

"Do you think I should wear a tie?" he questioned.

"No," she said irritably. "Your neck is too big, and you hate ties. You must be comfortable when you sing."

Amy showered, put on a matching set of lingerie, and applied her makeup. She dried her hair and pinned the sides back with decorative hair combs. She emerged from the bedroom, wearing a strapless periwinkle blue dress with matching high-heel sandals.

"Wow, you're gorgeous," he said. His approving smile told her everything she needed to know, and she blushed.

The final fourteen vocalists competed for the top six spots, three male and three female. The winners would get a chance to compete in Texas and be part of an elite group. All of the singers had spectacular voices, some good enough to make it to *American Idol.* Audience participation weighed considerably on the singer's scores, and they all invited friends and family to cheer for their performance. Ryan had told certain members of his family, but only two of his nieces attended. Though he had been clean almost a year, his family believed he was still a drug addict—a disappointing reality, but how could he blame them? He had to prove himself and regain their trust, which would be a slow road in the recovery process.

The house lights dimmed. A rainbow of lights circled the room. The spotlight beamed. Each vocalist sang two songs. Ryan chose "After the Lovin' " and ended his performance with Frank Sinatra's "Fly Me to the Moon." It would be the last time the judges made comments.

The first judge said, "I love you man, you're a Boston treasure. You're so engaging, and the thing I like most about you is that you're so real. You're just as real out there as you are on stage, and that comes across in your music. It has been a pleasure to meet you and hear you. Thank you."

"Hello, Ryan," said the female judge.

"Good evening," he replied.

"I liked that you filled in the gap of non-vocals in your second song with great dancing. It was fun to watch you. You're a great entertainer, and it was a lot of fun to watch and listen to you. You hit every note, and you were really just lovely. Thank you."

The second female judge remarked, "The thing I adore about you so much is that you make the music your own. I can hear that Boston accent in your songs, and I loved the dancing. I agree that you're certainly an entertainer, and I too, love to watch you. I love the way you take these old standards and make them 'the Ryan song.' Great job."

The MC announced the first-place winners. Ryan was not one of them. Amy held her breath. Ryan turned to her and said, "Forget about it. I know you're disappointed, but I'm sure I didn't make it. There are a lot of good singers here." The MC called the names of the second-place winners. Again, Ryan did not make it. Amy sighed and wanted to cry, but she held her composure for Ryan's sake.

"And now, finally, the third-place winners," the MC announced. The female winner was a young woman who sang like Whitney Houston. Amy crossed her fingers, and her feet for a bit of extra luck. She knew this was his last chance.

"Lastly," shouted the MC, "I would like to bring our third-place male winner to the stage. Ryan O'Connor, come on up and take your place with the other winners."

The place went crazy and the audience complimented him with a standing ovation. It was his first competition and his finest achievement. Ryan's mouth dropped to his stomach. Amy's frown turned to cries of joy. He received a hundred-dollar prize and an invitation to the National Karaoke contest. She quickly took a moment to compose herself and joined him on the dance floor for a victory dance. The sound of Johnny Mathis singing "Why Did I Choose You" filled the room, and the words stirred up something deep in their souls. He kissed her as they danced, and she melted away in his arms.

When the music stopped, he looked her in the eyes and said, "You look beautiful tonight. I'm so glad you talked me into finishing the contest. I love you so much." A slight tear welled up in his eye.

"I told you, and I love you, too," she whispered, and planted a firm kiss on his lips.

"By the way, are you in the mood tonight?" he asked, grinning from ear to ear with exciting pleasure.

"No," she said with a sexy giggle. "The two drinks I had aren't enough to put me in the mood, and three will make me too drunk."

"No problem—we'll split one," he suggested, a shrewd glaze in his eyes. They laughed heartily and left the dance floor. Ryan went to the bar and ordered another drink.

When they returned home, he cupped her face between his palms and kissed her hard on the lips.

He took her by the hand and walked her to the bed. He made slow, passionate love to her until they collapsed from exhaustion. When he finished, he pressed her face to his chest and hugged her tight. She fell asleep breathing in the mixed aroma of his sweat and Armani aftershave.

On Sunday morning they attended Christian services, followed by brunch at the Marriott Hotel. When they returned home, Ryan changed his clothes. He looked at Amy and said, "I have to go out. I'll be back soon."

Ryan did not return for an hour. When he finally appeared, she asked, "Where did you go?"

"I stopped by my mother's house and paid her some of the money I had borrowed over the years. Then I went by the pizza shop and made good on the check I bounced. Next payday I'll pay back some of the other checks I bounced."

"I'm so proud of you, Ryan." She rose from the couch, put her arms around him, and kissed him. "And I love you."

"I love you," he said, and bent down to kiss her again.

Ryan continued to sing three or four nights a week, and with practice he sang like a celebrity. He competed at the National Karaoke contest in Texas, but did not make the top ten, and it did not matter to him, because singing was his passion. He learned how well he could sing, and it was all he needed. The crack days disappeared forever, and he was a complete person for the first time in his life.

Ryan met a completely new set of friends,

leaving the dealers and crackheads behind him. As he found more friends and more karaoke clubs, he established a "favorites" list. One night Ryan and Amy met Mandy, a foxy barmaid at a club in Weymouth. Ryan fell in love with her, as did Amy. She was a hard-working single mother of five. Every Thursday night they visited her at the club. She loved the way he sang, and they all became close friends. It started a new, rewarding life with new friendships.

Early one Thursday night, when they returned from a visit with Mandy, the telephone rang.

"Hey man, it's Nokie. How are you doing?"

"I'm good man, what's up with you?" Ryan asked.

"Same old shit. I was in Quincy today. I drove by your house, but you weren't home."

"Yeah, I've been working," Ryan said.

"Been a while, I wanted to say hello. I left you a present in your mailbox," Nokie told him.

"Oh, that's cool man, but I'm finished doing that shit. Take it easy, brother." Ryan hung up and headed out the door to the mailbox.

"Where are you going?" Amy asked.

"Hold on, I'll be right back," he told her.

He returned to the living room a few minutes later with an envelope in his hand, "That was Nokie on the telephone. He told me he left us something in the mailbox."

"You're shitting me?" she said.

"Amy, think of all the money he made from us over the years. He's just trying to get our business back," Ryan added. "Don't worry, I let him know we're all done."

Amy followed Ryan through the kitchen to the bathroom. She thought she could talk him into cooking it. It was free, and one whack would not kill them. She watched him take the two forties from the envelope and throw them into the toilet.

As much as Amy wanted a whack, she watched the packages spiral down the toilet. In an instant, she knew they were going to make it.

The following week, he told Mandy about his former drug addiction. He told her about the packages Nokie left in the mailbox, and she bought Ryan and Amy a drink to celebrate.

Mandy was caught off-guard to learn how many years Ryan and Amy had smoked crack. "You're lucky you're still alive," she told him with a surprised glance.

Without hesitation Ryan responded, "I'm by far no holy roller, but a day doesn't go by where I don't thank the Lord for giving me a second chance," he said earnestly.

"My God, I would never have known you were a drug addict. You guys look pretty good for going through that many years of shit."

Ryan realized from his friendship with Mandy that they had one characteristic in common: they both knew family and friends always came first.

Ryan and Amy continued to visit Mandy at work and home. A few weeks later, she invited them to a barbecue to celebrate her daughter's high-school graduation. They became more like family than friends.

Over the next few months, they worked hard and saved money. Amy was two weeks ahead on every bill. She was not happy at the Oceania Hotel and wanted a change. She decided to look into reapplying for a position at the Milton Arms Hotel.

George Mills still owned it, and was willing to give her a second chance. He made her take a drug test, and she passed. He offered her the job of assistant manager on the day shift, for he knew that would be the best way to supervise her work performance. If there were any impropriety, George could deal with it on a personal level. She was a complete person again.

A month later, Ryan approached Amy. "I would like to celebrate our sobriety with a vacation."

"I like your thinking. Where do you want to go?" she asked.

"Let's have a second honeymoon, and go back to St. Maarten. We've saved enough money to afford a nice trip."

"Great idea. I'll have to see if Mr. Mills will give me a week vacation."

The following Monday, Amy asked George about a vacation. Since they were friends, he agreed. She started to pack the suitcases two weeks early. Ryan still needed to fix the relationship with his family, but decided to work on it when they returned from St. Maarten.

On an early morning in September, they took the Logan Express to the airport. They were so excited they arrived two hours early for the flight. They enjoyed a coffee and a muffin at Dunkin' Donuts and toured the newly renovated terminal.

They boarded a 727 at eight that morning. The steward strolled down the narrow aisle with the refreshment cart, and this time Ryan ordered a vodka and Cranberry while Amy settled for her usual Captain Morgan and Coke. The steward handed them the cute little mini-nips. When he started to open the juice can, Ryan stopped him. "Can I please have the whole can? I'd like to pour my own. Thank you."

"That goes for me too, please," Amy decided. They munched on the cookies and peanuts, slipped the headphones over their ears, and watched the in-flight movie.

With the advantage of a strong tailwind they began their descent into Princess Juliana International Airport ten minutes early. Ryan looked out the window several times as they closed in on the runway. "Hey, Amy, you gotta check this out," he told her.

Amy leaned over him to look out the small window. "Move your head a little to the left. I can't see." He did. "Wow, it's awesome. We are so close to the water. Shit, it looks like we're going to crash into the ocean." Squeezing their heads together made it easier for them to look out the tiny window. The 727 came within fifty feet of the white sandy beach, which was jammed with sunbathers.

"Wow, did you see that?" he asked Amy.

"Sure did. That was way too close for me," she said. They laughed nervously, and landed safely on the runway a few minutes later. They had brought one carry-on each, and Ryan grabbed them from the crowded overhead bin. As they walked down the rolling stairs that leaned against the airplane, the beautiful tropic breeze and warm sun embraced their faces. They quickly passed through St. Maarten Customs and hailed a minivan—otherwise known as a "taxi" in the Caribbean—to the Hotel Beach Resort.

The resort was a twenty-minute trip, and as the taxi stopped in front of the open foyer to the hotel, they saw the turquoise waves of the ocean crash down on the powdery white sand. Caribbean green marble spread across the floor of the foyer and down a spiral staircase to the beach. The hotel amplified the elegant Caribbean accents of teakwood lounge chairs with comfortable, cozy cushions of blue, green, and canary yellow. The airy lace curtains breathed in and out through the balmy breeze.

"Wow, baby, look at this place. It's heaven. We're going to have an awesome time. I'm so glad we stopped that shit." Ryan leaned down and kissing her.

She kissed him back and said, "You got that right. Look at all the things we've missed over the years."

"I know, baby, but it's all going to be different now. I love you."

"And I love you, too. Let's find our room and start a well-deserved vacation."

They opened the door to their room and found a complementary welcome basket of intoxicating tropical fruits. They threw the suitcases on the bed and stepped out onto the balcony, which overlooked an inviting crystal-blue pool. They immediately opened the suitcases and changed into their bathing suits.

"Are you ready?" Ryan asked Amy.

"Let's do it," she said as they walked hand-in-hand to the beach.

The hotel included three restaurants with their vacation package, and the first night they ate a five-course meal at the Italian Bistro. They joined other guests at the Tiki Bar and tried every cocktail, from a Piña Colada to a Hummingbird.

Later that night, Ryan and Amy returned to their room. He pushed a loose lock of hair from her petite forehead. Her knees wobbled, and her insides turned to mush. He placed a strong arm around her back and led her to the bed. He gently lifted her feet and laid her on the bed. He kissed her softly as his hands explored her body, and she melted into him as if they were one. He made slow-thrusting love to her, and they shuddered together in a climax. It was a first for both of them. It was a long time since they had taken real pleasure in each other's bodies.

After three nights, they tired of the hotel restaurants and ventured downtown. They ate dinner at a cute little French restaurant called *Les Escargots,* followed by another session of slow, passionate lovemaking. They made love most nights, reinvigorating their marriage.

At six o'clock the next morning, Ryan started the day with a Bloody Mary and made a pot of coffee for

Amy. He opened the sliding door to the balcony and settled into the patio chair with his cocktail. She sat beside him and sipped her coffee as they watched the island come to life.

The balcony faced the wharf in Phillipsburg, and as they sat quietly, watching the cruise ships dock, the glass slider to the adjoining balcony opened, and a middle-aged man appeared.

"Good morning," Ryan said.

"Good morning to you, too," said the man in a Canadian accent. "What a beautiful place."

"It doesn't get any better than this," Ryan said cheerfully.

"Eh. Where are you folks from?" the man asked as a woman joined him on the balcony.

"We are from Boston. Quincy, in fact. It is fifteen minutes south of Boston. How about you guys?"

"We are from Peterborough, Canada," the man said, extending his hand to Ryan, who rose from his chair and accepted it.

"I'm Ryan, and this is my wife Amy."

"Good morning," Amy said.

"I'm Terry, and this is my wife Shelley. We have two children, Matt and Kaleigh, but you know kids, they're still sleeping."

"What are you guys doing today?" Ryan asked.

"We scheduled an offshore snorkeling trip," said Terry. "We're going to enjoy a family day."

"Well, if we don't see you at dinner, have a great day," Ryan told him. "Tonight I thought I would try my luck at the casino and check out the karaoke bar.

I'm sure we'll see you around."

They all spent four glorious days of sunbathing by the pool and swimming in the warm bay. On the balcony each morning before starting the day, Ryan and Terry enjoyed the breakfast of champions—a snort of Canadian Rye. While Ryan and Amy relaxed, Terry and his family enjoyed all of the activities the island had to offer. They occasionally met at the pool bar and dinner.

During the day, Ryan and Amy would watch the crab races at the hotel beach, manage to take a half-day tour of the island, or walked downtown for some shopping. At night Ryan would sing all of his favorite songs to a crowd of happy-go-lucky tourists from around the globe at two karaoke venues he had found. After he participated in the karaoke competition at the hotel lounge, Amy and he would return to their room for some naughty sex.

On the first night of the competition, the MC said to each contestant, "Tell us your name and where you're from." When it was Ryan's turn, he said, "I'm Ryan, and I'm from Boston." He sang his songs, and the crowd loved him.

On the last night, Ryan invited Terry and his family to the show, and they happily attended. When the MC asked Ryan where he was from, this time he shouted to the crowd, "My name is Ryan, and I'm from Peterborough, Ontario." Terry and his family fell in love with Ryan as they rolled over in laughter. That night he won his second karaoke contest, and Amy and he became lifelong friends with Terry and his wife, who visited Boston that spring. Ryan and

Amy flew to Canada the following September.

On the day before they left Saint Maarten, they checked out the infamous Sunset Bar and Grill. "This is the place we flew over when we landed," he told her.

She pointed to the standing surfboard by the bar. "Hey, check that out," she said. "They have all the times and flights written on the board. That is so cool."

"Let's sit, have a drink, and watch for a while."

"Okay," she said with pleasure. They watched the airplanes fly within twenty feet of the crowded beach, drank several cocktails with friendly tourists, and recorded videos to download on Facebook. Before they left for the hotel, they split a cheeseburger and fries.

"As soon as we get home, I need to set things right with my family," he said.

"It'll take some time, and I'm sure we'll get through it if we just work together," she responded.

The next morning they packed their suitcases and, after seven glorious sun-filled days in the Caribbean, flew home Sunday afternoon, refreshed and ready to begin the life God meant them to live.

As the plane made the turn into Logan Airport, Ryan turned to Amy. "You know, I had such a great time, and my life with you gets better every day," he told her with warm sincerity. "Crack cocaine is the devil's secret weapon of lies. There are people who'll call us dirt-bags, losers and low-lives, but they'll never understand what it's like to go through what we've gone through."

"I know and we'll have to ignore those kinds of comments," she responded. "No one should judge another unless they possess the ability to see through the flesh and into the soul."

"You're right, baby, and it doesn't get any better than this!" he replied. "We may not have a lot, but we have what we need. I love you."

"And I love you, too."

Heather McCarthy

Epilogue

In the weeks and months after their vacation to Saint Maarten, Ryan and Amy began the necessary challenge of setting things right with his family. They did so by committing to staying clean and enjoying the normal activities life had to offer—all of the pleasures for which they had never had time while getting high had been their only priority in life.

Over the next year, they gradually earned confidence and trust from family and friends while continuing on their simple but long road of living their drug-free life day to day and attending weekly Narcotics Anonymous meetings. They had no more week-to-week excuses to revisit their old crack habits. They promptly attended all family gatherings when invited, and gradually more and more invitations were forthcoming. Ryan's family steadily noticed the improvement in their son's behavior and general health. His relationships with his family grew stronger with each passing day.

Ryan continues to work as a painter, and Mr. Mills promoted Amy to an unsupervised hotel manager position at the Milton Arms. Ryan and Amy use their income to make up for lost time by traveling twice a year to the Caribbean and diverse destinations. They attend church services every so often, followed by Sunday brunch at their favorite restaurant. They now love the theater and frequently attend musicals such as *The Phantom of the Opera* and *Les Misérables* at the Boston Opera House. Ryan continues to sing karaoke and perform in cabaret shows in his spare time, and is always buoyed by the applause and cheers he receives.

Ryan and Amy have hired a lawyer to make a one-time deal with the IRS for payment of back taxes, and they are currently submitting monthly payments. This was not a difficult transition to make, considering the five hundred dollars they had spent weekly on crack.

When you become straight, you inevitably lose contact with the drug dealers and other addicts you had known. Dennis and Linda are still addicted and no longer see Ryan and Amy. Lou calls Ryan and Amy once a year to check in, but they refuse to socialize with him. They have lost all contact with Nokie, whose whereabouts are still unknown. Since the beginning of this story, Ryan and Amy have lost six friends to drug overdoses.

Junior visited them a year after they became clean. Though they had known him for ten years as a drug dealer, he was also a legitimate businessman. When he dropped by their apartment one day and found them clean, he gave Ryan a big hug. He was glad to see them happy and drug-free.

Ryan and Amy have remained clean for five years, and are planning a trip to Italy in two years to celebrate their 25th wedding anniversary.

Made in the USA
Lexington, KY
21 October 2014